TEACHING AND TECHNIQUES IN TECHNICAL EDUCATION

Teaching and Techniques in Technical Education

Edited by

D.P. Giridhar

S.S. Bhavikatti • M.R. Kappali

A.V. Shivapur • Vinayak Bankapur

ANMOL PUBLICATIONS PVT. LTD.

NEW DELHI - 110 002 (INDIA)

ANMOL PUBLICATIONS PVT. LTD.
4374/4B, Ansari Road, Daryaganj
New Delhi - 110 002
Ph.: 23261597, 23278000
Visit us at: www.anmolpublications.com

Teaching and Techniques in Technical Education

First Published, 2005

ISBN 81-261-2290-0

PRINTED IN INDIA

Published by J.L. Kumar for Anmol Publications Pvt. Ltd., New Delhi - 110 002 and Printed at Mehra Offset Press, Delhi.

CONTENTS

THEME-C: RESEARCH AND TECHNICAL WRITING

THEME-D: INSTITUTION MANAGEMENT AND CO-CURRICULAR ACTIVITIES

THEME-E: GENERAL

FOREWORD*

Dr. K. Balaveera Reddy, Vice-Chancellor,
Visveswaraiah Technological University,
Belgaum, Karnataka.

Over the decades the quality of education seems to have failed to keep pace with the fast track expansion in its quantity. In the recent days, quality of education has become major concern for the policy makers in the country. Quality in educational context refers to the achievement of desired learning at the level of mastery and desired learning, in turn refers to a variety of competencies in the different areas of learning and life. It relate to what the learner has actually learnt. So in the ultimate analysis quality resides with the learner himself /herself and not outside.

Among the entire gamut of factors that influence quality of education, the most important is the teaching process as operationalised by the teacher. The quality of teaching and therefore of teachers have to work decisively for attainment of quality in higher education and hence its importance cannot be over emphasized. In most of the discussions on quality education, lack of dedication, motivation, commitment and competence in teachers invariably emerge as the dominant reasons responsible for producing poor quality teaching and education. Therefore, besides recruiting quality teachers, there is always a need to create among teachers sustained motivation and commitment for quality teaching and their competence have to be continually upgraded.

*Inaugural Address

Today, the faculty engaged in higher education is facing many challenges in the dispensation of teaching responsibilities. It is not merely the command over the subject and the communication ability that counts, the teacher in higher education has to be reached for facilitating, motivating and inspiring students in the acquisition of knowledge, skills, and values. Besides, teachers have to play a role in the development of the horizons of their respective disciplines by way of involving themselves voluntarily in research activities. To help teachers perform these roles successfully, their orientation towards the profession and its values, communication skills, use of media, evaluation procedures, process of academic and scientific enquiry etc is essential.

Faculty development would mean that process which is undertaken to bring about qualitative changes in the faculty to facilitate and improve the professional competence of individual faculty members in fulfilling their obligations to achieve goals and objectives of their institutions. Thus any faculty development intervention should fulfill the twin objectives of meeting harmoniously the individual and institutional needs whereby, on the one hand, the individual reaches higher level of satisfaction and motivation and on the other hand the institution is able to achieve goals of education at a higher standard and in order to be effective, it should be planned keeping a balanced view of both these integrated ends in mind.

Opportunities for faculty development which may result in qualitative improvement in education are varied and depending upon the specific objectives to be achieved at a point of time may be organized both internally with the college as well as externally outside the teacher's parent institutions.

For an effective implementation of the idea of faculty development and its successful management, the role of the managerial personnel in the institutions of higher learning like the Principal and HOD's can hardly be overemphasized. Their responsibility in this regard should encompass the following:

- Visualizing the staff development needs of their teachers,
- Making themselves aware of the suitable avenues already available or to be arranged for fulfilment of these needs,
- Disseminating these information among the faculty,
- Motivating them to join the programmes arranged internally or externally,
- Providing necessary administrative and financial support,
- Evolving and implementing a mechanism to evaluate the implementation of new learning by the faculty members and its impact on learning and performance of students,
- Taking up any follow up action to strengthen the faculty development programmes and its good effects on quality of education.

PREFACE

Dr. S. S. Bhavikatti

It is often said "Teachers are born, not made". But the statement is not true in the present day context. There is a teacher in everybody and this aspect can be developed by proper training. Coolidge said 'few men are lacking in capacity, but many fail because they are lacking in application'. Hence any person, who has liking for the teaching profession, can become an effective teacher. The present day policy is 'Education for all'. Hence there is need for training a large number of teachers and such faculty development programmes are desirable. On the theme teaching learning process seven papers are presented in this workshop.

It is said,

- We think students want education, but they want degree.
- We think they want degree, but all they want is a job.
- We think they want job, but all they want is money.

Though this is said in lighter sense, there is nothing wrong to earn more money by legal means. Nobody will give the money, without doing job properly and nobody gives the job without having appropriate qualification and nobody gives degree without being educated properly. Though the awarding degree based on examinations is criticized often, no other system better than this is evolved. There may be some modifications in the system, but examination system remains the time tested means of evaluation. Good marks scored consistently by a candidate show his intellectual ability and his commitment to the duty assigned to him. Hence the teachers have to train the students to face the examinations. We have received seven papers in this area.

An academically excellent teacher is always respected by students, which in turn help the students to learn more. If we have obsolete teachers, we will get only obsolete pass out, we will have only obsolete technology and performance. Sri C. Subramanyam, the former governor of Maharashtra said, 'The teachers should be inspired by a burning desire to pursue the path of learning and keep abreast with the latest developments and advances in the subjects they teach'. Unless they themselves are embedded with a sense of learning, dedication and missionary zeal, they will neither be able to inspire the students nor bring out the best in them. Hence a teacher has to keep on improving his knowledge and teaching technique. I am glad to inform you that we have received five papers for this workshop in the field of research and technical writing.

Mrs. Indira Gandhi said, 'Ability is not always gauged by examinations'. Rajmohan Gandhi said, 'When brought together, Indian erupts in dispute, while the Japanese performs wonders'. Hence there is need to train our students not only for competence but for commitment and team work. These qualities can be imparted by co-curricular activities. There is need to balance curricular and co-curricular activities and manage them well. Proper management of institutions is also very important. Hence this has been incorporated as one of the main themes of the workshop. We have received five numbers of papers in this field.

To cover any other aspect of technical teaching, papers were invited on general topics in Engineering Education. We have received thirteen papers in this field.

The presence of dignitaries, deliveries by resource persons Dr. K. Balakrishnan, SDM Institute for Management Development, Mysore, Dr. H. P. Kincha, Indian Institute of Science, Bangalore and Sri Premanand Shetty, Executive Officer, SDM Education Society, Dharwad, and paper presentations by the faculty of SDMCET generated considerable interesting discussions. This workshop was restricted only to SDMCET faculty. However encouraged by the overwhelming response, we have decided to bring out the proceeding including discussions which will be beneficial to entire teaching community and in turn benefit students and the institutions.

MESSAGE—I

I am happy to learn that a 3 days workshop on "Faculty Development" has been planned by our SDMCET in which a number of papers are going to be presented on academics, managing co-curricular activities and orienting the students to face examinations.

I am also happy to note that the workshop is going to be inaugurated by the Vice Chancellor of VTU Dr. K. Balaveera Reddy and is getting resource persons from SDM IMD Mysore and I.I.Sc. Bangalore. It is heartening to note that 30-35 papers are going to be presented by SDMCET faculty itself. The papers by resource persons and the faculty of SDMCET may generate useful discussions and follow up actions to improve academic ambience.

I congratulate SDMCET for initiating such exercise and wish the workshop a grand success.

May lord Manjunathaswamy bless you all.

(DR. D.VEERENDRA HEGGADE)
President,
S.D.M.E. Society

MESSAGE—II

Dear Sri Giridhar,

We are extremely happy to note that SDM College of Engineering and Technology, Dharwad is organizing a workshop on Faculty Development on 26th, 27th and 28th of August at Dharwad which will be inaugurated by Hon'ble Vice-Chancellor of VTU, Dr. Balaveera Reddy.

The theme of the workshop i.e. Improving the Academic Standards, Co-curricular Activities and their management and orienting the students for examination, is very apt in the present scenario and these are to be taken up seriously by any Institution to maintain high standard of Education.

It is also heartening to note that good numbers of papers are going to be presented by our faculty during the workshop. We are confident that these papers will be of immense value for the overall growth of the Institution.

May Lord Manjunatha Swamy Bless the occasion.

Yours Sincerely,

(D. HARSHENDRA KUMAR)
Secretary,
S.D.M.E. Society

THEME A

TEACHING-LEARNING PROCESS

1

EFFECTIVE TEACHING: STRATEGIES, METHODS, TECHNIQUES AND ACTION PLANS

DR. MRITYUNJAYA V. LATTE

Asst. Prof., E&C Dept
S.D.M. College of Engg. & Tech.,
Dharwad- 580002

DR. N.H. AYACHIT

Prof. & HOD, Physics
S.D.M. College of Engg. & Tech.,
Dharwad- 580002

ABSTRACT

Technological improvements in the processes of the transfer of information have made a great demand on strategies of teaching–learning processes. Use of modern gadgets and the resultant communication revolution have made the world smaller in its dimensions from the point of view of access to knowledge. This has made the transfer of information through lectures ineffective. Keeping in the fact that lecturing as a strategy for transfer of knowledge has several impacts on the learner and that some of them have been lost because of the type of knowledge revolution that the present youth are going through. There is an equal and urgent need for newer strategies to be introduced in the scholastic learning systems of a classroom. The success of the strategy and methods will depend upon the different techniques used. Each technique has its own action plans. There is no doubt that there is a pressing need for taking a fresh look at effective teaching through new strategies, methods, techniques and action plans.

Introduction

Howard Gardner, in 'The Unschooled Mind', refers to three types of education—intuitive, experimental and scholastic [1]. In his comments on the disadvantages of discarding the first two and concentrating on the last, he goes on to establish the need for redesigning the strategies, methods and techniques adopted in the conduct of scholastic education. Gary Yuki, in 'Leadership in Organizations', stresses the need for developing all three Skills—technical, conceptual and human relations [2]. A tertiary teacher belongs to the last category and therefore human relations skills are more important than the first two.

Noam Chomsky, in 'Power and Prospects', refers to the influence processes of communication [3]. Undoubtedly, a teacher is next in power to the parents in influencing any scholar. The teacher is a classroom leader. The knowledge and use of different techniques of performing in the classroom need to be evaluated to understand the significance of their impacts on the classroom performance of the tertiary teacher. Hence it is important that a teacher's technical skill of managing a classroom is enhanced for greater effectiveness. Stephen Covey, in 'Principle-centered Leadership', has some comments to offer to all intellectual performers [4]. An intellectual performer needs communication skills and many of them are different from those of artistic performers, though both perform on the platform. The former needs, primarily, public speaking skills. However the technical skill to plan and execute the methods to be adopted in the intellectual interventions has a very great bearing on the intellectual performance while speaking from the platform. The methods adopted or the techniques used ought to influence the learner not only to listen, but also to participate by interacting with the teacher and, among and between other learners. Hence, the teacher's competence to perform in the classroom needs greater amount of development.

Roger Soder, in 'The Language of Leadership', explains the persuasive impact of leader effectiveness and deals with the three levels of intellectual influence through communication—Understanding, learning and enlightenment [5]. Debra Niehoff tells us in 'The Biology of Violence', that one reason for violent responses to situations is the boredom associated with routine life and its consequential impact on the style of living [6]. The boredom associated with the methods used by the lecturers in the classroom today, especially the policing of the youth into silence for considerably long periods, can be responsible for violent responses from students.

Lecture Concept 1

A full-length lecture can take listener into a confused state of mind apart from boring him to distraction. Very often, students do not properly understand classes on concept definitions or clarifications. Most of them reproduce these in examinations after studying by writing practice. Indeed in these cases there is no learning process at work at all. Therefore there is a need to use a different strategy and plan different methods that are to be adopted to achieve both.

Any lecture becomes meaningful to a student when a lecture plan is available to him. When a student is aware of the lecture plan he is able to plan himself for the listening processes as well as note taking processes. The self-confidence of lecturer will allow possible interactions at this stage.

Lecture Concept 2

A lecture is concluded not when it is delivered but when it has been comprehended. The language used, the explications offered, the examples presented and the skills of platform performance help a listening scholar comprehend not only the theme, but also its associated thoughts.

A successful lecture has to evaluate every lecture that he

delivers. Speechmakers are generally satisfied with their own delivery and the associated silence or a cheering response. In fact both need not indicate the listeners' comprehension except partially or in patches. Sometimes it is necessary that making a restatement of important points either through a summing up or through a written support make the comprehension complete.

Lecture Concept 3

The lecture as a method, as in most cases in Indian tertiary education, has only one associated written work that of taking down dictated notes. There are number of arguments that are provided by traditional lecture-giving teachers in favor of dictating notes. They say it helps the students to reemphasize what had been heard during the lecture, acquire speed in writing, the matter can be recalled faster during the examinations and even improve handwriting. Many of these are necessary skills, but not necessarily to be developed through writing down notes that are dictated in the class.

It is said that no adult can concentrate on a monologue for more than eighteen to twenty minutes, and they say, it is ten to twelve minutes for children. If someone wants to continue a monologue, the speaker will have to break it after eighteen to twenty minutes, interact or bring a diversion, and thereafter he may go on for another twenty minutes. What is to be stressed here is that the break has to be a designed one, so that it comes within the grip of a teacher.

Lecture Concept 4

A lecture has its limitations of being a one-way communication strategy. A lecture with questions designed for clarification towards the end of it has a better impact than a question-answer session, which may not clear all the students' doubts, either because of lack of time or because of lack of skill in both. Therefore, discussion, one may call it a clarification or removing of confusion or additional matter or even a repetition, recollection or interaction; is an important part of any lecture. Speaking for fifty percent of one hour lecture and using the remaining time to dictate notes does not constitute in its truest sense. Every subject taught has several themes to be brought to the cognitive domains of the student and theme-centered discussions during a lecture hour produce the best of cognitive influences.

Lecture Concept 5

Every tertiary teacher believes strongly in his ability to lecture the students to silence. Even his superiors will be satisfied with this towering teacher, whose powerful rhetoric creates an appreciation of the lecture. The success is attributed to the intellectual abilities, hardly realizing that it has completely killed both, the teacher and the student in the sense of the nullification of the artistic influence on the thinking processes.

A lecture not only influences that part of the intelligence, which deals with rationality and logicality, but also with other part of the intelligence, which deals with feelings and emotions. Hence if intellectual influences are always being made with an emphasis on rationality and logicality, the areas of feelings and emotions are likely to suffer. Therefore from this point of view of a lecture, an intellectual intervention ought to make use of the strategy of artistic trials towards achieving learning.

Lecture Concept 6

Very few lecturers are capable of recognizing a very simple truth that some of the students can be more brilliant than the teacher himself, even when the teacher is more knowledgeable and hence more powerful in a classroom situation. If the ultimate objective of the lecturer is to offer the best to the students, then the classroom strategies, which he adopts, should not rest with his best. He should go over to a possible engineering of the class's best. If this is the objective, then, the most brilliant in the class should be asked to produce the best out of him for the benefit of the entire class. The popular belief of lecturers that anything beyond the syllabus is not necessarily a matter for the students is very unfortunate. It is true that from the point of view of an examination the lecturer is correct. But, after all, the objective of the tertiary education is not a mere pass or grade in an examination. When a teacher is able to take the students beyond the curriculum or syllabus, he serves the objectives of taking a student to personal or resource effectiveness. Every attempt by the lecturer to empower a student with conceptual clarity and development of associated skills is also going to decide the leader effectiveness of the student.

Lecture Concept 7

Listening to a lecture is primarily meant for comprehending the content of the lecture, either to accept or to reject the ideas. It is also possible that a lecture has an influence on the listener beyond an ordinary understanding. They may influence the person even to make necessary changes in his systems, habits or discipline of life. These are the intellectual influence processes that may be the direct results of a lecture.

Conclusions

A teacher is a classroom leader, leading a group of wards to learning, to development of skills and to resource effectiveness. Teacher empowerment alone can guarantee innovations. If we need quality we have to innovate. The sooner we try, the better the education we provide.

REFERENCES

1. Howard Gardner, 'The unschooled Mind'
2. Gary Yuki, in 'Leadership in Organizations'
3. Noam Chomsky, in 'Power and Prospects'
4. Stephen Covey, in 'Principle-centered Leadership'
5. Roger Soder, in 'The Language of Leadership'
6. Debra Niehoff in 'The Biology of Violence'.

DISCUSSIONS

Q: Is it right to expect perfect silence in classroom?

A: Not for the full period. It can be perfect silence for 18-20 minutes. Then there can be little diversion but this should be in the grip of the teacher..

Q: Should there be diversions from subject matter?

A: No. Instead it can be in the form of questions on portion covered till then.

Q: How about using new teaching aids like IT tools.

A: Aids can be used. However teaching is more a "one to one" process and hence direct lecturing in classroom is better.

Q: What if the student is better than faculty in subject?

A: Faculty should not have inhibition to consult such student.

Q: Maintaining one type of lecturing for 18-20 minutes– is it not too long duration?

A: It can be tackled by breaking monologue in systematic way.

Q: Class has heterogeneous mass. Who is to be kept in mind for teaching?

A: It is to be the average student.

Q: If every thing is available on-line due to recent IT tools, then what teacher has to do?

A: Classroom lecturing is better in my opinion.

2

TECHNIQUE OF TEACHING

Mrs. Savitri Raju
Asst. Professor, E&C Dept.,
SDM College of Engg. & Tech.,
Dharwad -580 002.

ABSTRACT

Teaching can be deadly monotonous or delightful. It almost entirely depends upon the extent to which you can use your imagination. This article attempts to identify some of those important aspects that make teaching different from coaching. Maintaining a perspective and communicating into the student are most important tasks of a teacher over and above the repetition and the driver recovered to communicate knowledge to a class. The instructor should well plan the entire subject. Prepare thoroughly. Be flexible. Be prompt.

Before the Term Begins

The *instructor* should layout the plan for the entire term, in the light of the objectives of the subject and its relation to the curriculum. He must guard against chronic under estimates of the time required for the students to grasp a given topic. The order of presentation should be from familiar to the unfamiliar, from simple to the complex, from that which is easy to that which is most difficult.

Plan in advance for *quizzes* to be given at the time of continuity breaks between topics. About Five percent of the allotted class time is usually adequate for testing purposes.

During the first week of the term give unmarked quiz covering the prerequisites of the subject.

In the class room the physical comfort of the students and of the instructor is important if full attention is to be centered on the subject matter. Inspect your classroom before the term begins.

Before Each Lecture or Recitation

Prepare adequate notes and master them so that an occasional glance is the most help you will need from them. Think thorough – or actually rehearse – the subject matter, order and manner of presentation. Do not be ashamed to rehearse. It is worth your time. Obviously, written out lecture is not to be read to the class. The text should probably not even be brought to the classroom. Thoroughness of preparation is what is wanted.

If you have previously taught the same material, criticize yourself. Look for improved approaches to the subject, which will make it more stimulating to both the students and yourself. The most practical way of doing this is to write comments to yourself on your lecture directly after giving it. When you come to it next year, these comments will remind you to the changes which you should make.

Do not try to cover too much material at the expense of clarity and complete comprehension. Plan provocative questions and illustrative problems and situations in order to stimulate the student's interest, oral discussion and critical evaluation of the subject. Do not be too quick to help a student who is struggling with a problem. He may have to muddle around in a subject for quite a while before it becomes clear to him. This muddling process is at the core of all creative thinking.

Be flexible, use a variety of techniques of presentation –

lecture, recitation, discussion, demonstration or other methods as the circumstance indicates. You must interest yourself in the student as much as in the material and you must learn to be sensitive to slight and subtle changes in the student's attitudes and personal reactions. Level your attention and planning at individual students, not to the class as an impersonal body of people. Develop a warm, friendly relationship in the student instructor team. Practice the habit of calling students by name whether in classroom or corridor.

At Each Meeting of the Class

Be prompt. Have ready any exhibits, slides and papers to be distributed or used. Be pleasant, cooperative, and sincere. Begin with a short review connecting the previous class work with the new material you intend to present. To learn effectively and efficiently, the student must first have the desire to learn. He will have the desire if he understands why the new material is important and if he feels that he is making steady progress that he is getting somewhere.

"It is only by varied reiteration that unfamiliar truths are forced upon reluctant minds".

In teaching, try to appeal to as many of the receptor senses as possible. Among the five senses (sight, touch, hearing, taste & smell), the most effective in the learning process usually is sight. Retention is generally poor from hearing, if unaccompanied by other stimuli. It is for this reason that lecture material is much more readily understood, absorbed and retained if the lecture makes effective use of the black board, of models and other visual stimuli while speaking. Use models if available. Motion pictures with sound are excellent because they appeal simultaneously through sight and hearing.

If a speaker has to proceed without any of the teaching aids, and has to rely on voice only, then at least learn to use hands and facial expressions both in holding interest and attention and in the actual process of conveying ideas. Homework assignments should be planned carefully in advance. They should be illustrative to the current work, with an occasional review problem thrown in to breakup the crank – grinding state of mind, which commonly results from a number of problems on the same topic.

3

A CASE FOR USING MODERN MANAGEMENT CONCEPTS TO BRING-IN ATTITUDINAL TRANSFORMATION IN TEACHING

Dr. Shashidhar S. Bhavikatti
Professor & Head, Dept. of Chemical Engg.,
S.D.M. College of Engg. and Tech.,
Dharwar-580 002.

ABSTRACT

Globalization of the world economy has opened up new opportunities as well as challenges and threats in all walks of life, whether one is in business or in education field. While globalization has resulted in the creation of increased number of jobs in the developing world, particularly in the technical field in India, it has posed fresh challenges to the academic institutions. The academic standards have to be vastly upgraded to produce more number of "Global Engineers". In this context, the role of teachers engaged in technical education is becoming more and more challenging and they have to gear up to upgrade their skills to face such competition. Modern management concepts such as TQM, Kaizen, etc have been able to improve the efficiency and effectiveness of the corporate sector. The manager in the corporate sector has improved his performance by learning communication skills, time-management skills and SWOT analysis. The teacher can also adopt similar strategy and employ some of these concepts to improve his performance and survive in the fast changing scenario in the field of technical education. This paper highlights a few of these concepts that are relevant to the teacher and help him in improving his attitude towards teaching and the students, apart from increasing his effectiveness.

Introduction

Globalization means different things to different people. The most common understanding is the growing interdependence and interconnectedness of the modern world. The increased ease of movement of goods, services, capital and information across borders through technological advances has created a truly global economy. What happens in one part of the world affects our own security, our prosperity and the way we live our daily lives, whatever be our profession. The field of education is not in any way isolated from these developments. India has a comparative advantage over other countries in terms of large pool of scientific and engineering manpower as result of which we are the biggest beneficiaries of outsourcing of jobs from the developed world, particularly in technical field. To consolidate these benefits further, our engineering colleges need to produce world-class engineers which can only happen if the teaching has to match the international standard. This is a time when each teacher is required to carry out his own SWOT analysis and improve his teaching skills. In this context, it is worth noting that the corporate sector reengineered itself with number of modern management concepts to improve its efficiency and effectiveness to face the competition due to globalization and survive in the market. What the managers in the corporate sector have done for their survival can be replicated by the teachers as well in the developing world so as to produce more number of *global engineers*. The word "Global engineer" is coined here to represent those engineers with sound technical knowledge in their field of specialization, excellent language and communication skills, adaptable to work in cross-cultural surroundings and reasonably immune to hire-and-fire policies.

Changing Scenario of Technical Education and its Impact: Indian Perspective

Education in the country is becoming market driven and today we are witnessing increasing number of unaided colleges entering education field. In the forefront are the engineering colleges as the software development field has opened up unprecedented demand for engineering graduates. The demand for engineers is not just restricted to software field alone. Industry leaders with diverse background, such as the Reliance Group, Dr. Reddy's Labs, Bharti Telecom Industries, etc., are entering education field with the objective of producing engineering graduates suited to their own line of activities. In the coming years, tie-ups with foreign universities are bound to take place, which would help in the international recognition for Indian degrees. Considering the fact that the cost of living as well as the fee structure in education is quite low compared to western countries, we can foresee the influx of foreign students in the years ahead. Such developments would pose new opportunities as well as challenges to the teachers in the country. The ones with good teaching skills could expect better job opportunities and increase in their remunerations, while the others may have to take VRS and retire from the service as has been the case in the Banking and Manufacturing sectors.

In order to manage the inevitable process of change and survive, the teacher has to make many attitudinal changes towards the students and teaching. In this context, adopting some basic management concepts like customer orientation, Kaizen and TQM as well as acquiring new skills such as effective communication, time management, SWOT analysis, etc will help the teacher in improving his performance as they have helped the managers in corporate sector. This paper attempts to highlight how some of these concepts can be applied to teaching profession.

Concept of Customer Satisfaction

Customer satisfaction is one of the main concepts that the businesses adopted to improve their performances. Customer satisfaction was considered as a critical component of profitability that ensures the customer stays with the company longer, deepens his relationship with the company. A satisfied customer recommends company's products and services to others. To extend this concept to teaching, first we have to define who our customers are. For a teacher, the student is the first and foremost customer. One of the effective ways of improving our attitude towards students would be through the introduction of the concept of "customer comes first" to serve them better. On the top of the agenda for the teacher would be to strive to satisfy the needs of the students. However we should not interpret this statement to mean that what the students want is to pass the examination with least effort and teacher should facilitate this process. Basically one can look at the student as a raw material and at the end of four years of stay in the engineering colleges, he gets converted into product, i.e. engineering graduate. We have to realize that there is another important customer whom we have to satisfy, that is the employer who is going to hire the services of engineering graduate. So the education has to be aimed at producing right quality graduate with character who is well-equipped to meet the challenges awaiting him in the real life. A satisfied customer, in our case, the outgoing student recommends our institution to others and helps in building the reputation that facilitates attracting new students. Similarly the satisfied employers keep returning to the campus for campus interviews. In this context, we need to believe that our livelihood is based on the quality of the product, i.e., the quality of the students that we deliver. If this concept is clear in the minds of the teachers, their attitude will see a sea-change and will be appropriate to facilitate improvement in the relationship between the student and the teacher.

Kaizen and Total Quality Management (TQM)

These are some of the widely practiced Japanese management concepts in the corporate sector worldwide. According to the management guru and the Chairman of Kaizen institute Masaki Imai "Japanese management practices succeed simply because they are good management practices. This success has little to do with cultural factors. And they lack natural bias means that these practices can be-and are-just as successfully employed elsewhere". We could stretch this statement further to mean that with appropriate innovative interpretations these practices can be applied to the academic field.

Kaizen means "improvement" and the Kaizen strategy calls for never-ending efforts for improvement involving everyone in the organization. Not to be satisfied with the status quo is a virtue in Kaizen philosophy. Further Kaizen also signifies small improvements as a coordinated effort by all the employees in the organization, i.e. it emphasizes team work in any endeavor. The starting point for Kaizen is setting the right mindset and applying it to academic environment, calls for continuous improvement in the academic standards based on customer driven strategy leading to customer satisfaction, which in our case means satisfying the students' needs, their parents' aspirations and the prospective employers' expectations. The process oriented thinking as opposed to result oriented thinking propagated by Kaizen in our case means we have to concentrate on the activities involved in producing quality engineering graduates and not just look for good results in the final year examination. This means that we have to work towards creating opportunity for industrial training, personality development, extra curricular activities, inculcating self discipline in the students apart from regular class room teaching to equip them to face the real life.

The Total Quality Management (TQM) calls for shared vision and the activities for each employee in the institution including top management should be geared towards achieving the same. If people in an organization do not have the same purpose, the organization will be weak. Applied to academic institution, TQM calls for integrated effort involving not just the teachers but also all other employees of the institution such as those working in the administration, hostel management, Industry-Institute Partnership Cell (IIPC), HRD, Placement centre to improve their performance to satisfy the customers, primarily the students and the employers.

Time Management Skills

As a teacher one is expected, apart from class-room teaching, to involve in innumerable activities, ranging from guiding the students in their project work; carrying out own research work and publishing papers; pursuing higher studies; net-working with other teachers and researchers in the field of interest; attending workshops and seminars; presenting research papers; valuation work; consulting work; counseling of students to routine administration work.

The time management skills are some of the most important career skills that one can learn. They involve learning of practical techniques for time-management that are essential for successful people in different walks of life. The teacher too can benefit immensely as they help him in becoming reliable and effective. They show him how to identify and focus on the activities that give the greatest returns. They explain the method of goal-setting, which is a vitally important skill to achieve ones' ambitions in his life. At the core of time management concept is an important shift in focus which encourages concentrating on the results and not on just being busy. Many people achieve very little success as they spend more time on trivial things and don't concentrate on the right things.

The technique of time-management involves costing ones' time, deciding work priorities, making activity list, prioritizing them and scheduling them. Here the time-management tools help in deciding the priorities, coming out with action plans, tackling the right tasks first (Prioritized "To Do "Lists), effective scheduling. Effective time-management essentially requires the knowledge of the purpose of the job and identifying the measures of success.

Today there are a number of time-management tools available that include diaries, calendars, paper-based organizers, software suites like MS Outlook etc. But one doesn't have to wait for procuring appropriate software. What is essential is awareness that one needs to better manage his time and he can start with manual prioritized "To-do" list. Every morning one should prepare the To-Do list for the day and before closing the day, he should review how much he has achieved. This itself will substantially improve the efficiency as well as increase the will power. It is a good idea to begin with list of tasks that are reasonably achievable during the day and progressively include the complicated ones in case one has a weak will power. The daily To-Do list should be in line with the overall objectives and goals one would like to achieve in longer term.

SWOT analysis

It involves analyzing oneself for his strength (S), weakness (W), opportunity (O), and threat (T). It helps in developing self-awareness that can be proactively used to improve oneself. This analysis comes handy to the teacher as well as anybody else. Some of the parameters against which the teacher could evaluate himself are: Whether I have good communication skill; How deep is my knowledge of the subject; How do I perceive my personality and how do the students perceive it; Whether I have good command over language; Whether I manage my time well; Whether I am able to build good rapport with the students; Whether I am keeping abreast with latest developments in my field of specialization, whether I am spending enough time in research activities, publishing papers, etc. We can add many more to this list.

The analysis would involve asking appropriate questions and coming out with appropriate answers. This involves the following steps:

Strengths: What advantages do I have? What do I do well? What relevant resources do I have access to? What do other people see as my strengths?

Weaknesses: What could I improve? What do I do badly? What should I avoid? Do other people seem to perceive weaknesses that I do not see?

Opportunities: Where are the opportunities knocking at me? How to capitalize them?

Threats: What obstacles do I face? Is changing technology making me redundant? Could any of my weaknesses seriously threaten me professionally?

Carrying out such analysis will often be illuminating - both in terms of pointing out what needs to be done, and in putting problems into perspective.

Effective Communication

Key ingredient of good teaching is effective communication and the greatest single stumbling block to real communication is the one-sided nature of speaking. A well organized lecture prepared with students' perspective coupled with an interactive method of delivering lecture with enthusiasm should generate enough curiosity among the students and accepted by them as a good lecture. Avoiding monotonous voice and use of visual aids, wherever required, would also be helpful in effective communication Creating rapport with the students is vital to being accepted as a good teacher which means one should be able to build a sustainable relationship of mutual trust, harmony and understanding. Effective counseling may be one of the important means in developing rapport with the students. It involves the understanding and fulfilling the needs of the student. Everyone needs at least one person with whom he can freely discuss his personal problems and will be affected by the happenings, desires, fears - of their life. The student is no exception and craves for appreciation, recognition and respect. A little compliment at every opportunity and genuine concern in his well being will go a long way in his well being and help in building the rapport.

Conclusions

The academic institutions and the teachers involved in technical education will benefit immensely by applying modern management concepts and be able to upgrade the academic standards in the developing countries to the international level. This will result in the production of "Global Engineers" in sufficient numbers to meet the growing demands of the international employment market.

REFERENCES

1. www.quickmba.com
2. www.1000ventures.com

DISCUSSIONS

Q: Technology and corresponding problems being country / region specific how much relevant is your idea of "Global Engineer"?

A: Today we are living in a world in which any happening in any part of the world is going to affect us directly or indirectly and truly we are approaching era of 'Global Village'.

Unfortunately we don't have choice of being isolated from the globalization phenomenon. Today's buzzword is 'either globalize or perish'. In this context, global engineer is called upon to address to the problems of the world, whether the problem concerns the developed world or the developing world. The more number of global engineers we produce, more services the country will be able to offer to others and this benefits more.

Q: "Proper attitude towards students" means what?

A: It means treating the students as our valued customer. Identifying the needs of the students and satisfying them should be our first priority. This will result in appropriate grooming of the student and enable him satisfy the needs of his customer namely his employer. All this calls for effective partnership between the student and the teacher. The attitudinal changes brought in through such thinking will bring about appropriate transformation in the mindset of the teacher and will automatically result in right response in innumerable types of situations he will be encountering in his students. It is not necessary to elaborately list out how exactly to behave in particular situations.

4

ROLE OF TEACHERS AND MODERN IT TOOLS TO IMPART NEED BASED EDUCATION TO ENGINEERING STUDENTS

Dr. H.G. Gopal
Professor & Head, Dept. of E&E,
S.D.M. College of Engg. & Tech.,
Dharwad- 580 002

ABSTRACT

Today, engineering education has become a commercial commodity. Prime stake holders are looking for appropriate engineering education that fetches them good job and helps them to prosper in the field. Unplanned growth in professional colleges and hike in fee structure is keeping students away from professional education itself. Added to this, there is lot of competition among the professional institutions to attract students. In such situation, students are all looking for need based education. Role of engineering teachers are crucial and they have to train their students to meet the new challenges. In this regard modern IT tools come for the teachers rescue. These issues are discussed in this paper.

1. Preamble

In the new century, capacity of people to learn and continue to learn throughout their life describes a country's wealth. To enhance this capacity of learning, education is quite important. Education as per Webster dictionary is the process of developing the knowledge, skill, mind, character etc [1]. Any education is meaningful when it preaches ethical values to any individual to produce an integrated personality, an integrated development of skills, head and heart. In Indian context, education is always focused on the development of holistic society. Seers and sages of this country have left a mine of wealth on the value system for any one to imbibe, cultivate and prosper [2]. Coming to engineering education, it has a vital role to

(a) provide general curriculum for our technological culture,
(b) bridge the gap between traditional curricula and the needs of modern age,
(c) display its specific concepts for use in other disciplines and
(d) spawn new academic areas of study.

Many of these academic areas have emerged as amalgamations between engineering and other fields. Philosophy of engineering education does not change with time. Hundred years from now, one may still be emphasizing the same points. Prof. William H. Burr rightly pointed these facts 110 yeas ago as the more we change, the more we remain the same. Entry of many global players (MNCs, business magnets etc) to the Indian market has led the Indian entrepreneurs to unprecedented challenges from across the globe. In the wake of this stiff global competition, every student is looking for need based education that not only moulds him/her to be fit for the modern industrial needs, but also leads him/her to the sustainability in this globalization challenges.

2. Challenges Faced by the Present Technical Education System

The overall percentage of placement of fresh engineering

graduates both from campus and off campus selection reveal the fact that many industries are recruiting fresher only after he/she possesses some additional skills apart from the knowledge imparted in colleges. Finishing schools after graduation are gaining lot of importance and the parents are also keen on this type of training, as it fetches their wards a lucrative job. These additional training to a fast learning student is ok, but for a slow learner it poses lot of stress. As a result, these students are segregated in the society. For example, University subject experts and great educationists propose 5 theory subjects and 2 or 3 laboratories for each semester, based on the learning rate analyses. Now because of the global challenge, every student will learn one or two computer languages apart from his regular studies (in many cases, parents force them to go for tuitions also!). This will pave way for slow learners to loose interest in the regular curricula. It is rightly said in Khatopanishath, "How many lamps one can light with limited oil? Even if one serves, how long these lamps glow?"

In this context, today education is not complete, after a student leaves the college with basic degree. Even those who are successful in getting a job are also subjected to this type of training and this is at the cost of their employers. To day every student is aware of these facts and he/she always looks for an opportunity of this kind during the studies or vacation. Keeping this in mind, engineering education is required to be remolded considering the overemphasis on generalization and adding specifics within chosen optional boundaries. Different aspects of vocational training and industry-institute interaction which would inculcate a sense of managing things by themselves in younger generation need greater emphasis.

It is therefore time to make reforms in engineering education considering the two most important components:

(i) which is invariant across different countries, dealing with basic sciences, engineering sciences, etc and

(ii) in tune with the national goals of economic and industrial developments that includes electives, projects, humanities, social sciences, appropriate technology subjects etc.

Adequate emphasis is required to be given on professional skills, attitudes, individual needs and the challenge of accelerating technological change to meet the global competitiveness.

3. Modern Information Technology Tools

Conventional education methodologies involve, in majority of the cases, only one sensory organ of the students to grasp and in few cases two! Research in Education Technology reveals that involvement of more sensory organs (2 or more) quadruples the learning rate. In this context, traditional education methodologies are not adequate for the new challenges of the time. With explosion of technology and easy access to internet, the culture of learning has shifted from the traditional way to one that is boundless and time invariant. To deliver the educational programs, Information Technology tools are being increasingly co-opted in the new learning environment. This enables man-to-man communication coupled with the ability to (a) store, (b) search and (c) generate enormous amount of meaningful information.

Proper use of audio conferencing, interactive video conferencing & computer mediated communication, computer/web based training and virtual class room concepts motivate slow learners come to regular stream or to the level of expectation fast. For example, both students and teachers feel subjects like power plant technology, switchgear and protection etc as boring because either there is not much analytical treatment is involved in these subjects or the subject is totally imaginative. Majority of student community feel Electrical Engineering is tough as they can not see voltage, current or power, though they are using electricity in their day to day life! Elementary laboratory to train students on the application of electricity is also eliminated from the curriculum based on this feeling! When the author experimented this technique with the help of UGC and other embassies to teach Power Plant Technology to students using multi media based CDs (on hydel, thermal, nuclear and renewable power with every point visualized through (i) working models or multimedia based animated diagrams, (ii) working video clippings, (iii) interview with the experts and local people), the result was marvelous. All the students visited these power plants voluntarily after their examinations and expressed their joy! With minimum expenditure such wonders are possible only through IT tools.

Relatively, present day students are well informed and exposed to the new technology as use of computers and internet is included in the school curriculum since five years. They have used multimedia to study many things such as, solar system, principle of rocket launching, nuclear fission and fusion etc in high schools.

Students should be encouraged to prepare small write-ups on few topics with in the subject by visiting to websites of other Universities, Industries and Journals. This assignment motivates them not only to understand the basics on their own but also drives them deep into the subject. For this purpose, teacher may have to give a small weightage in the internal assessment (by asking few questions in the monthly tests on their assignment itself).

4. Role of Teachers in the Present Scenario

As mentioned above, today students are well informed about the available technological tools. In this context, role of teachers in engineering education needs total transformation from teacher driven methodologies(wherein teacher is given a prime role in teaching learning process and the student is merely a recipient of the knowledge dished out by the teacher[3]) to student centered methodologies. Here the two key words to describe learning are behavioral change and practice. Learning styles are the typical ways a person behave, feel and process information in learning situations. It describes how a student learns. Different students prefer to study differently. This learning technique changes from subject to subject! Role of teacher here is to understand the learning styles of his students and orient his lessons in that direction using modern IT tools. This demands a drastic behavioral change even in teachers also. Indeed teacher has to change from learn-teach philosophy to learn-teach while practice–learn more philosophy. This is what our Hindu mythology preaches through OM, the first lesson taught by our parents. That is a change from Mananena Upasana to Upasanena Manana, i.e., transformation from application after understanding to understanding through application! Teachers must update their knowledge every time. They must visit different web sites regularly and if possible make field trips in addition to regular learning through books and journals. Vocational industrial training can also be taken up if possible. Before transferring QIP from plan scheme to non plan scheme by the state Government, training fresh engineering teachers at TTTIs and/or in industries for 2-3 months was compulsory to get their probationary declared. Due to lack of funds and interest from the management of professional institutions this scheme was dropped. Continuous interaction with the industry will also help teachers to update their knowledge.

Teachers can organize summer / winter vocational classes to their students to mould them according to the industrial expectations. This is indeed quite important as the majority of the industries in India and abroad is quite dissatisfied with the level of preparation of graduates they recruit and feel that institutions have failed in their objective of imparting the relevant education. Regular meeting with industrial experts, inviting them to colleges to give lectures on advanced fields and taking joint student & staff projects will help in this direction. For this, University curricula and regulations should provide enough freedom to the teachers. It is better to involve industrial experts while framing the syllabi for engineering. If not, feed back from industrial experts must be taken before adopting the final syllabi.

For all these to realize, teachers must have enough enthusiasm and they must preserve the same enthusiasm and motivation right from the day one to his superannuation. This is the real bottle neck, as teachers become sensitive year after year, due to constant human interaction, delayed financial benefits, promotions and personal problems etc. Managements of professional institutions must think in this direction and take possible remedial steps to ease out this unrest. Simple things like appreciation to their efforts, reduction in other work loads, sharing organizational/managerial responsibilities, offering books/computers/better working atmosphere for their achievements etc, will solve majority of the unrest. This will catalyze teachers to share the additional load with more vigor.

Finally, cooperation from both students and their parents is equally important for the success of imparting need based engineering education. They must participate actively while identifying the industrial needs and in the engineering education program by giving proper feedbacks. In some cases, parents themselves can promote the industry institute interaction in identifying the industrial needs and placement through their personal contacts.

5. Final Word

An attempt has been made in this paper to address the importance of need based education and role of IT tools in this direction along with the role of teachers, student and parents. It is indeed crucial to impart need based engineering education. Competition among professional colleges put a real challenge for rural or interiorly placed engineering institutions to get away from this problem. As such teachers must play a vital role using modern IT tools to realize today's engineering students expectations and finally to visualize Vasudeva kutumbham.

ACKNOWLEDGEMENT

Author wishes to thank the authorities of SDMCET, Dharwad, for encouraging him to conduct survey in this area and to write this article.

BIBLIOGRAPHY

1. *Webster's English Dictionary.*
2. Sudarssanam, "Human values in Technical Education", *IJTE,* vol. 25, no 4, Oct – Dec 2002, pp 1-7
3. R. Hariharan, "Information Technology for teaching and learning", *IJTE,* vol. 25, no 4 Oct – Dec 2002, pp 29-33.
4. Summary of few slokas from Khatopanishath
5. Personal experience in TTTI training at TTTI, Chennai.

5

SOME ASPECTS OF ACADEMICALLY WEAK STUDENTS AND A NOVEL METHOD OF IMPROVING THEM

Mrityunjaya Kappali
Asst. Professor, Dept. of E&E,
S.D.M. College of Engg. & Tech.,
Dharwad – 580 002.

ABSTRACT

Due to prevailing privatization of education and stiff competition, very sustainability and proper development of an engineering college demands high academic ranking, which is decided mainly by its performance in examinations. Academically weak students affect this performance adversely. Hence they need to be improved. This paper discusses about the causes and effects of weak students. A novel method of improving them is proposed and implemented. This involves conducting weekend tests along with scanning of student class-notes. It's observed that there is remarkable improvement in their written presentation with over 90% of students scoring more than 15 in IA and passing final examination.

1. Introduction

In the present days of privatization of education and stiff competition, very sustainability and proper development of an engineering college demands better quality and adequate quantity of student in-flow. For this, the college has to have high academic ranking, which is decided mainly by its performance in examinations. Thus performance in examination turns out to be an important index of merit for the college. Many factors affect adversely this index e.g.: poor infrastructure, academically weak students, poor teaching etc. These are to be tackled and set right.

Of these 'academically weak students" is a major factor. Their poor performance in examinations brings down the overall result of the entire college. Hence it's necessary that they be improved. Also avoiding or minimizing their failing in examinations, enables them to devote more time for co-curricular activities, which enhances their career prospects. This paper discusses about the causes and effects of weak students. A novel method of improving them is proposed with special emphasis on their theory internal assessment (IA) score and written presentation. This involves conducting weekend tests along with scanning of individual student class-notes. The proposed method is implemented on 4 batches of students. The results are found to be encouraging. Their written presentation improved remarkably. The number of students scoring more than 15 in IA and passing final exam is above 90%.

2. Weak Students

"Weakness" parse is not absolute. It is to be associated with a specific attribute. In an engineering college, weak students can be thought of as those with poor academic performance, indicated by their IA/ university examination (UE) results. In this paper those scoring less than 15 in IA are considered as weak.

2.1 *Significance of IA Marks*

Our university (VTU) prescribes 125 marks for each subject (theory as well as practical) out of which 25 are for IA and 100 for UE. It does not prescribe any minimum score in IA for theory but stipulates that for passing, the total minimum score is to be 50 out of 125 with a minimum of 35 in UE. One can attend UE even with zero score in IA but should score at least 50 in UE to pass. This is tough job for average and below average students for some difficult subjects. Instead with a target of bare minimum 35 marks in UE, which most of the students can make, one has to have minimum 15 in IA making total 50 for a pass. It's observed that many students fail in theory subjects even after scoring 45 and above in UE just because they don't have required IA to make total 50. Hence safe approach for the students would be to score at least 15 in IA of each theory subject.

2.2 *Effects of Weak Students*

Weak students pose a problem to themselves as well as to faculty, college and society at large because of the following reasons:

(a) Due to weak students the examination results decrease and hence the ranking of concerned faculty and the college as a whole will drop. This affects adversely the fresh admissions to the college.

(b) Weak students usually exhibit lack of concentration and involvement in the class proceedings. Hence become possible sources of indiscipline. Being slow learners, they will act as speed breakers for classroom teaching.

(c) After repeated failures, they might end up dropping the course itself. This means all the efforts, time and money spent on them till then are in vain which is a national waste.

2.3 *Causes and Remedial Measures*

Students become academically weak and do not perform well in examinations due to different reasons mentioned below:

(a) Neglecting classroom teaching – not even maintaining class notes properly – lack of regular studies – over confidence – trying to do self-study, that too at the semester end. All this leads to average score less than 15 in IA & poor performance in UE.

(b) Poor written presentation – lack of neat, systematic, structured, appropriate writing in IA test/ examination answer papers.

(c) Basically poor intellectual ability –inability to follow the subjects at a faster rate.

The weak students can be improved by the following measures:

(a) Improving their IA score – making it at least 15.

(b) Improving their written presentation.

(c) Instilling confidence and motivating them to take interest in class proceedings.

This demands, from the faculty, tremendous patience, compassion and understanding towards them.

3. Proposed Method

This is meant for theory subjects. Here at the end of each week, on Saturday, teacher conducts a simple test of one-hour duration "Week End Test (WET)" for the subject he is handling, on the portion covered in that weak. The questions are of brief answer type. When the test is going on, the teacher scans the subject notebook of each student to find: Is it neat? All the class work is noted? Problems / numericals given for homework are solved? Missing class portion is noted & learnt? etc. Simple comments with date & signature are written on the first page of the notebook like: "OK, Writing to be Neat, Date, Margin, Title, Diagram".

The answer sheets are valued making suitable corrections & returned to the students in the very next class. The teacher discusses in the class about general mistakes committed, improvements necessary, etc. Students understand opportunities for improvements.

Every week, there is a proof that he/she is doing well. It's a strong motivation to continue doing well. This procedure, continued over many weeks sincerely, improves their written presentation & subject understanding. Such improvements observed are mentioned in the class with an appreciation. The question papers are given to them so that they will have good collection of questions acting as question bank.

4. Implementation of Proposed Method

The proposed method has been implemented for 4 subjects in 4 different semesters (batch codes: B1, B2, B3, &B4). The details like subject, class, WET's taken, IA& final examination results etc. are given in Table1.The details of a batch of students without implementing proposed method is given in Table 2. This batch can be taken as reference batch (BR). Comparing the results in Table1 with those of Table 2, indicates the effectiveness of the proposed method.

5. Results

(a) Students became more sincere & attentive in the classroom proceedings. Better discipline in the class.

(b) Written presentation improved remarkably. It became more neat, structured and appropriate. It was a pleasure seeing this transformation.

(c) IA performance improved with the number of week students dropping to less than 10% (Fig.1). UE results improved significantly with the passing rate increasing to above 90% (Fig.2)

(d) "Passing" fulfilled, some students devoted time and efforts for co-curricular activities enhancing their career prospects. Increase in students' morale was quite visible.

6. Critical Comments

(a) As it's optional, general attendance is not very good. This may be made compulsory with the support of the college authorities & the parents.

(b) If extended for all subjects, it will over burden the students. It's advisable to implement it on need basis.

(c) It gives an impression of over-caring with a risk that students feel their passing is the responsibility of the faculty! But, for at least some batches with large number of weak students, it is necessary.

(d) There will be additional load on the faculty. However such overloads are inevitable in result oriented work environment.

(e) The whole exercise, though aiming at more marks, has the basic intention of inculcating "better written presentation, regular work, disciplined approach" as an attitude in the students.

7. Conclusions

Performance in examinations is an important index of merit for an engineering college. Academically weak students affect this performance adversely. Hence it's necessary that they be improved. Also their failing in examinations is to be avoided or minimized so that they can devote more time for some co-curricular activities enhancing their career prospects. Present paper discusses about the causes and effects regarding weak students. A novel method of improving them is proposed with special emphasis on their theory internal assessment score and written presentation. This involves conducting weekend tests along with scanning of individual student class-notes. The proposed method has been implemented on 4 batches of students. The results are found to be encouraging. Their written presentation improved remarkably. The number of students scoring more than 15 in IA and those passing final examination are both above 90%.

8. Acknowledgement

The author thanks the authorities of SDMCET, Dharwad for all the support extended in the implementation of the proposed method of improving the weak students.

TABLE 1

Details of Batches Implementing Proposed Method

Batch Code	*Class & year*	*Subject*	*Total strength*	*Students with<15 score*				*Final*
				IAI	*IAII*	*IAIII*	*Average*	*passing*
BR	I Sem Sept. 1999	Electrical Sciences	54	42	13	15	14 (26%)	70% (38/54)

TABLE 2

Details of Reference Batch (Proposed Method Not Implemented)

Batch Code		*B1*	*B2*	*B3*	*B4*
Class & year		II Sem March 01	IV (E&E) March 03	V (E&E) Sept. 03.	IV (E&E) March 04
Subject		Electrical Sciences	DC & Synch. Machines	Power Electronics	Power Electronics
Total strength		66	49	48	65
Number of WET's held		4	6	4	4
WET Attendance		25	27	46	44
Students with < 15 score in IA	IA-I	22	31	6	12
	IA-II	26	9	29	28
	IA-III	28	9	8	8
	Average	6 (9%)	3 (6%)	0 (0%)	3 (5%)
Final passing result		83% (55/66)	96% (47/49)	92%(44/48)	Awaited

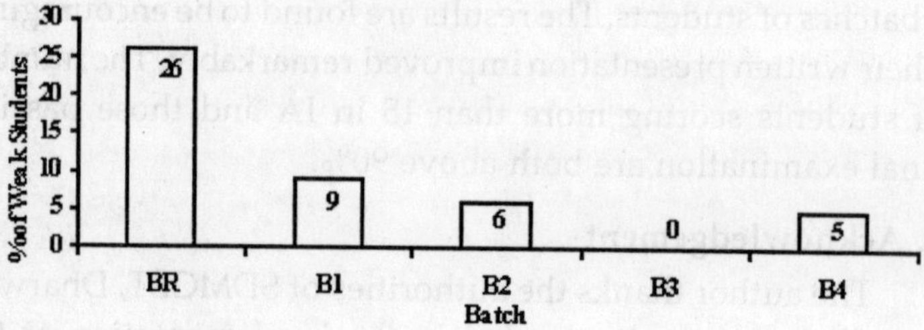

Fig. 1. %of Weak Students vs. Batch

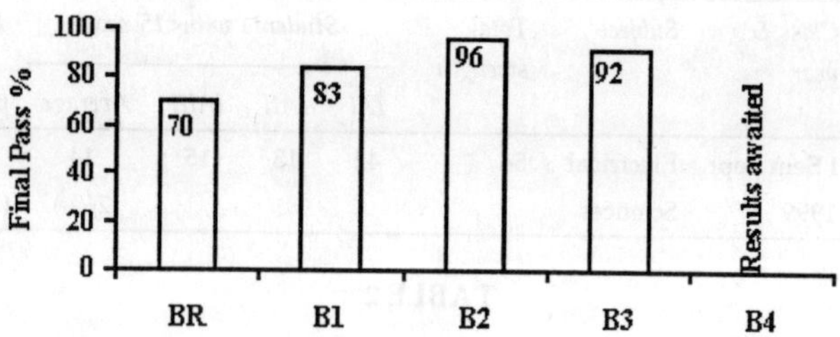

Fig. 2. Final Pass % vs. Batch

DISCUSSIONS

Q: What are the reasons for the students to be weak according to your observations?

A: The reasons are both global and local ones. We have effect of society, parents, type of grooming at home and earlier schooling under global category. Local reasons are student related like lack of concentration, sincerity, hard work, intellectual ability, right self-assessment etc.

Q: How far IA marks reflect student's weakness?

A: IA marks are not absolute indicators of weakness. However, in general, score in IA gives a hint about the attitude of the student like work culture, subject understanding, regularity, written presentation etc. Hence scoring low IA marks can be generally assumed to be an indicator of student's weakness.

Q: Do you expect the students to score IA marks or do we have to give IA marks?

A: Not we giving. We should motivate & prepare the students to score IA marks themselves.

Q: Is it not too late if students are assessed through IA, as the first IA is only after a month.

A: Conduct a weekend test much before the first IA or identify weak students based on previous semester results.

Q: Have you made any observations on overall performance of the students in your experiment?

A: Yes I have made. There is improvement in overall academic performance as well as overall personality. Since the approach here is at attitudinal level, the positive qualities gained will be reflected in other subjects also thus improving the overall academic performance. Clearing the subjects makes the students feel more confident. He/she can devote time for co curricular activities which improves his/her overall personality.

6

READING METHODOLOGY

Vijaya C
Asst. Professor, E&C Dept.,
S.D.M. College of Engg. & Tech.,
Dharwad -580 002.

ABSTRACT

Reading is the most important academic skill and the foundation for all academic learning. If we do not read, we are on the road to academic failure. Reading is the other side of writing. It is to writing what hearing is to speaking. Virtually any form of writing is a kind of notation and any form of reading is a type of performance [3]. A contemporary reader reading silently will hear an inner voice, which may call up inner sight. A good reading will inculcate good mental habits in good readers who are, therefore, more apt to be understanding, compassionate, sympathetic, and empathic with respect to their fellow human beings than are bad readers or even non-readers, for that matter. Unfortunately a good number of readers, usually discouraged by the length of works, skip over reading. To help counter this and other obstacles to reading, understanding, and enjoying reading, let me present the reading methodology.

1. Introduction

The relation between writer and reader is illustrated in figure below [6].

Every text is produced by an actual writer (a real person), who in the act of writing automatically places in the text a version of him/herself, the implied writer. What may not be so obvious at first is that the implied writer automatically creates a mirror image of another person, the implied reader, which the actual reader reading the text in question is implicitly asked to play along with. Both writing and reading are, in fact, acts—that is, roles that writers and readers voluntarily take on [6].

Figure

The difference between an actual writer and an implied writer is that the latter is text-bound whereas the former is not [6]. The actual writer is outside the text and the implied writer is inside the text and will live forever there, as long as copies of the text exist and will come to *"life"* again in the reader's imagination each time the text is read.

The concept of the implied reader may be a bit more difficult to grasp. In some opening of the text there is addressing to the readers directly [6]. Reading those opening words should make us immediately cognizant of who we are supposed to be as we begin to read the book. The point is that we begin by assuming the role of the implied reader. By doing this we are actually cooperating playing along both with the actual and implied writer.

However, the readers have the right to anything, the right to reread, the right to read anywhere, the right not to read, the right to skip pages, the right to not finish, and the right to escapism, the right to browse, the right to read out loud and the right not to defend your tastes. [2]

2. Select What You Want to Read

Knowing what you want to know is the first thing to ask yourself. Why you are reading the text? Are you reading with a purpose or just for pleasure? What do you want to know after reading it? Once you know this, you can examine the text to see whether it is going to move you towards this goal. [1]

For this you need to do a preview which normally takes 30 to 60 seconds [4]. Say you have a book in your hand. Look over the title of the chapters. The introduction should let you know whom the book is targeted at, and what it seeks to achieve. Look at all the headings, subheadings and marked, italic or dark print. Chapter headings will give you an overall view of the structure of the subject. Look at any pictures or illustrations, charts or graphs or maps. They are there to make a point and hence don't miss them. Quickly skim over the passage, reading the first and last paragraph and glancing at the first sentence of every other paragraph.

Where you only need the shallowest knowledge of the subject, you can skim material. Here you read only chapter headings, introductions and summaries. If you need a moderate level of information on a subject, then you can scan the text. Here you read the chapter introductions and summaries in detail. At this level of looking at the document it is worth paying attention to diagrams and graphs [5].

Close the book and ask yourself [5]- what is the main idea? What kind of writing is it? What is the author's purpose? Ask yourself whether the book meets your needs and if it assumes too much or too little knowledge. You might not think that you could possibly answer these questions with so little exposure to the material, but if you do the preview correctly, you should have some very good general ideas. If you have a general idea of what the passage is about before you really read it, you will be able to understand and remember the passage better. You will improve your comprehension if you somehow "preview" the passage before you actually sit down and read every word.

3. Start Reading

Create questions from your reading to help your mind think about the material. Look at each section at a time and turn the boldface headings into, as many questions as you think will be answered in that section [4,5]. The better the questions, the better your understanding will be. You may always add more questions as you continue. When your mind is actively searching for answers to questions, it is learning. Here's an example. If a heading says "classification of signals," you can make a question like: "How signals are classified?". "Microprocessor" can be a question like "Why the name Microprocessor and what is its purpose?". Make up as many questions as you possibly can.

You must remember that you are reading it in order to get something from it and ultimately from its writer who has worked for you, for your benefit. Good readers are capable of putting aside their own egos for the duration of the act of reading. Reading a chapter correctly takes a lot more time. Study time rule for class says that 1 hour of class requires 2 hours of study time. This reading method will seem slow at first, but the benefits will soon be clear. You will remember more of what you read, and you won't waste time repeating work you've already done.

If you want to read well, you must pay attention. There is a lot more to reading well, but paying attention is an unavoidable first step [4,5]. If you are not paying attention, you might as well stop reading, for you are no longer registering what is being said, which means that you have already stopped reading anyway. Just looking at the words won't do. A single careful, attentive reading may not be enough for full comprehension, but is often more effective than constant regressions in the middle of a reading. It is best to work on paying closer attention the first time through.

For those technical articles that are particularly long, make a list of major technical words. The list should include the different forms of the name, systems, filters etc. for example and the relation they have to one another. As you work through the technical article, keep the list close by for quick reference. Different sorts of documents hold information in different places and in different ways. They have different depths and breadths of coverage. By understanding the layout of the material you are reading, you can extract useful information much more efficiently. A good way of recognizing this is to compile your own table of contents before you open the document. You can then use this table of contents to read the document in the order that you want. You will be able to spot omissions quickly.

Usually it is best to make notes on knowing what you need to know and reading appropriately, knowing how deeply to read the document- skimming, scanning or studying. Using active reading techniques pick out key points and keep your mind focused on the material.

As you read, look for the answers to the questions you put at the beginning, and write the answers in your notes [4].

Read each section of the chapter with your questions in mind. Look for the answers. When you finally get to the point where you are actually slowly reading the passage, read in a "questioning" manner -as if you were searching for something. Now you have a goal; something to look for; something to find out. When you are goal-oriented, you are more likely to reach the goal. At least you'll remember one thing about the text, which you have just read.

Stop talking to yourself when you read [4]. People talk to themselves in 2 ways, by vocalizing, which is the actual moving of your lips as you read, and sub vocalizing, which is talking to yourself in your head as you silently read. Both of these will slow you down to the point in which you find that you can't read any faster than you can speak. Reading should be an activity, which involves only the eyes and the brain. Vocalization ties reading to actual speaking. Try to think of reading as if you were looking at a landscape, a panorama of ideas, rather than looking at the rocks at your feet.

Studies have shown that when we read, our eyes must make small stops along the line [4]. Poor readers make many eye stops than good readers. Not only does this slow you down, but also it inhibits comprehension because meaning is easier to pull from groups of words rather than from individual words or even single letters. Try to read in phrases of three or four words, especially in complete clauses and prepositional phrases. Your mind may internalize them as if the whole phrase is like one big meaning-rich word.

Vary the speed of reading [4] to suit the varying difficulty in the content of the article that you come across while reading. Poor readers always read at the same slow rate. An efficient reader speeds up for easier material and slows down for the hard. Some things are not meant to be read quickly at all.

Principles discussed, derivations of important results are very difficult text and should be read slowly. Easier material and magazines and newspapers can be read quickly.

When you are reading a document in detail, it often helps if you highlight, underline and annotate it as you go on [5]. This emphasizes information in your mind, and helps you to review important points later. Doing this also helps to keep your mind focused on the material and stops it wandering. This is obviously only something to do if you own the document. If you find that active reading helps, then it may be worth photocopying information in more expensive texts. You can then read and mark the photocopies. As you progress through the article, make notes at the top of the page regarding certain important derivations, theorems or conclusions. This will make reviewing previous derivations or conclusions less time consuming. In addition one can review the derivations or conclusions at a glance and get a better idea of the overall text content. This makes the work "smaller" and easier to understand.

See all that's in a text and no more than what's in a text. If you make a mistake at this level, you are likely to distort the entire context of a given text. In other words, if you see something in a text that's not there, you are adding something to what you are reading, so that you are no longer reading the text you think you are reading. One technical term for a mistake at this level is "irrelevant association".

A corollary of this idea is the notion that what's in a text is plenty for you to work with. In other words, there is no point in seeing things that are not there. One way of avoiding any sort of erroneous association made with something said in a text is not only to pay attention to what is really being talked about in the text, but also not to jump to conclusions prematurely. Don't assume that you understand what a writer means until you have completed reading the entire text. It is, of course, impossible not to make tentative guesses or hypotheses as to the meaning of the whole fairly early on in the reading process, but remember to remain both open and flexible-minded nevertheless. Be ready, in other words, to adjust your sense of what a text is all about as you go along.

After each section of reading, stop, think about your questions, and see if you can answer them from memory. If not, look back again (as often as necessary) but don't go on to the next section until you can say what you have learned. Once you've finished the entire chapter using the steps above, go back over all the questions that you made. See if you can still answer them. If you cannot, read the chapter again, being careful to answer your own questions.

If possible discuss with others what you read. This increases comprehension and retention. After reading a particularly long or challenging section replay the events and conclusions in your head. Go back to the book if something doesn't make sense. It is beneficial to remember a summary of what you have just read.

4. Enhance Speed of Reading

For most people, it is easy to learn to read faster. Your reading rate is often just a matter of habit. But to begin, you may need to try to change some habits when you read and you read as if it really matters. Most people read in the same way that they watch television, i.e. in an inattentive, passive way. Reading takes effort and you must make the effort. A wise teacher once told me that you can learn anything if you do three things: pay attention, pay attention and pay attention.

Twenty or thirty minutes and four or more times a week is generally better than reading for several hours once a week [7]. Follow up the article main aim appearing in other articles or in subsequent magazines for several days. At first this may seem difficult, but it will become much easier and more interesting as you become familiar with this technique of reading. You will quickly notice, for example, that certain key words are repeated almost in every article, making them easy to learn and difficult to forget.

5. Conclusion

In order to truly read, we must re-write the book with its author. Good reading breeds unselfishness. Good readers develop good listening habits, too. In an essay titled "What is Art" Tolstoy defines art as, "One man consciously, by means of certain external signs, hands on to others the feelings he has lived through, so that others are infected by these feelings and also experience them. ... If I were told that what I shall write will be read in twenty years by the children of today and that they will weep and smile over it and will fall in love with life, I would devote all my life and all my strengths to it". Thus when writers love to put life time efforts into writing and enjoy writing, let us employ the reading methodology discussed in this paper to read, understand, gain knowledge and enjoy what is written in books and articles.

REFERENCES

1. Study Skills from English-Zone.Com
2. Pennac, Daniel, *Better Than Life*, Coach House Press, 1996
3. Notation and The Art Of Reading by Karl Young
4. Institute of multi-sensory education California Task Force on Reading, Every Child a Reader
5. Mind tools e-book Review By James Manktelow
6. The Art of Reading Steven C. Scheer
7. Bankok Post Educational Services: Tips on reading a newspaper for EFL and ESL learners (NiE).htm

DISCUSSIONS

Q: What's the difference between reading with purpose and that for pleasure?

A: Reading with a specific objective, for knowledge is reading with purpose. e.g.: Technical reading.

Reading for entertainment – light reading – is reading for pleasure. e.g.: Reading during traveling.

7

PRACTICAL IMPLEMENTATION OF THEORETICAL ASPECTS

L. Krishnananda
Faculty, E&C Dept.,
S.D.M. College of Engg. & Tech.,
Dharwad -580 002.

ABSTRACT

Author discusses in this paper about the significance of mathematical relations and algorithm on the implementation of theoretical aspects in teaching. He also emphasizes on the need to introduce high end machines and use of software in regular curriculum.

Introduction

- Best way to learn things is doing it.
- Learn the concepts well. Try to understand the significance of a Mathematical relation, or a Boolean equation or an algorithm.
- Know complete details of the topic to be learnt through discussions, Books and the Net.

Steps Followed

- While teaching in the class room, focus on the importance of a topic in real life situations or any other practical / useful implementation. For ex: while dealing with " Filter design" one can try to give the usage of it in communication area or a simple " Graphic Equalizer" in an MP3 or radio broadcasting. Similarly for subjects like Microprocessors or Microcontrollers, many examples like washing machines, Digital camera, fire alarm systems etc. can be demonstrated.

- Give the list of applications for the concerned topic and ask the students to think about different applications related to the particular algorithm or device you are discussing. This gives you sometime to dwell on the topic as well as students would be more focused in the classroom.
- Certain topics definitely need more insight and elaboration than others. Take the case of teaching MS-EXCEL to students. You can ask them to design Bar charts for different real time examples like population, scores obtained in exams etc. For teaching DBMS, illustration of banking transactions could be an ideal example.

Breaking the Ice

- Subjects like Image Processing, Networking, WEB Design, etc. require intuition and thinking on part of the students. This requires extensive laboratory or demo examples to illustrate the concepts. Hence simulation of the problems using tools like MATLAB, FPGA Advantage etc should be given as exercise in addition to the theoretical concepts.
- For subjects that require exclusive lab support, Lab manuals should be prepared in advance. Along with regular set of experiments, additional questions can be given for each set to give more practical exposure.
- A set of questions related to the particular topic

can be given to the students in advance and hints can be given in the class for solving these problems. For eg. While teaching 555 TIMER, special applications like pulse stretching, frequency division, Pulse Width Modulation could be discussed.

- Some of the concepts can be developed as a Mini Project or could be given as an assignment to the students during vacation.
- For teaching latest topics faculty should be trained. In this regard, separate budget allocation is to be made for each department. Training for the faculty in the emerging areas like Embedded Systems, Web Technologies, VLSI Design, MEMS, etc. is essential to impart knowledge to the students and also to keep updated according to the industry needs. Hence, a comprehensive faculty development policy is to be planned at the earliest.

THEME B

EXAMINATON AND EVALUATION

8

INTERNAL ASSESSMENT - ITS ROLE, CHARACTERISTICS & PROBLEMS

Dr. G. Neeraja Rani
Department of Physics
S.D.M. College of Engg. & Tech.,
Dharwad – 580 002

Dr. N. H. Ayachit
Department of Physics
S.D.M. College of Engg. & Tech.,
Dharwad – 580 002

ABSTRACT

Bloom the great educationalist observed that in our country, there is no system of education but a system of examination. This is mainly; true in case of INTERNAL ASSESSMENT (IA) which was introduced as per the National Policies on Education NPE 196k Internal Assessment which gives way to continuous assessment is expected to do a let in educating the students,, for their understanding of finer parts of syllabi. The expectations of IA, its characteristics and problems associated are discussed in the article presented, with an idea to bring out a discussion on how to improve the same.

Aim of Introducing Internal Assessment (IA)

- To remove the undue emphasis on the final examination as the sole determinant of success.
- To integrate teaching and evaluation and to test

those skills that cannot be tested through a written examination at the end of the course.

- To help the teacher in getting more and better information about the students Knowledge, Intellectual abilities, Skills, Interest, Initiative, Discipline, Attitudes, Aspirations they want to develop according to their performance in their IA.
- Also for the teachers to change their style of teaching so that, a better understanding of the subject is made available to the students.
- In other words the continuous evaluation (IA) not only shows the ability of the students also evaluates the ability with which a teacher transfers knowledge to the students and adopt accordingly.

Characteristics

- Internal Assessment is a continuous periodic and internal assessment is done in relation to certain abilities and skills in certain subject areas periodically and continuously. Syllabus interpretation and clarifying objectives of learning has to be planned at the time of curriculum development. The assessment has to be done by the teacher of the subject in the institute only and not by any external agency.
- IA does not mean only a few mid term examination in the place of final exam but has a pert to play in a planned evaluation system and is taken as a part of the final exam.

IA demand that the outcomes of learning a particular subject must be spelt out first and then the choice of suitable, meaningful, valid and reliable evaluation tools to match these abilities and skills are made.

In IA very low weightage must be given to simple recall of knowledge and information.

To serve as a feed back it must generate a lot of information to improve teaching learning process.

IA marks or grades must be made known to the students immediately after evaluation is done and the results are to be discussed with them individually.

The results must be studied statistically and an effort must be made to improve the system.

Important is that there should be reduction in time between holding exams and declaring results.

Giving weightage to IA and end exam is another important factor which has to be looked in very care fully, because it can boost the percentage of marks of the students. Recently this study has been done by Dr. N. H. Ayachit et. al. and published in a paper. In which it has been shown that IA and practical marks are not at all in consistent with the theory marks scored by the students

Problems

No Uniformity In courses: Whatever a teacher teaches in the class room is final. In view of this we find that the performance of a particular batch of students in the university examination does not match with internal assessment marks. Therefore it is necessary to have a moderation of IA books from some external person as per the contents of the question paper.

Topics are as guide lines and levels of questions: The type of the question paper for the internal assessment purely depends upon the teacher. This can be used for the students' advantage. However in practice people feel, it is being used such that it is disadvantageous to the students. Please note that the disadvantage doesn't mean harassing the students by giving tough questions and less marks, it should be understood as by giving easy questions and more marks with out giving a proper importance to the contents and depth of the subject in- fact the student is at disadvantage. In view of this it is necessary that uniformity is brought by mentioning the amount of syllabi covered, by fixing the number of questions with different marks depending upon the theory part or problem part. Probably this can be achieved by creating a proper question bank for the university with some flexibility as far as the numericals is concerned. This type of things may bring uniformity not only between different batches but also between different colleges. However one should be cautious about the books in the form of guides coming out for even these question banks.

Attitude of Students Towards Teachers

The IA in its original scope is supposed to bring a good interaction between student and the teacher because of his accessibility for mode of evaluation. But one has to be doubtful whether this is happening in real sense. This is because the transparency in IA evaluation is to bring out the attitude of a student. Although we talk of an open society neither students nor teacher are in real sense so. This has kept a distance between teacher and the student. It may be experienced that when a teacher deliberately does a trivial mistake students do not respond in spite of repeatedly asking whether they have understood or not or any mistake in the derivation and so on. This is probably true with every teacher and it is not because of the teachers fault in general although may be true in one or two cases. But, these one or two cases which creates a phobia in the minds of the students and avoid them coming out not only connected with the problems associated with IA but in general. Contrary to the very expectation of introduction of IA in the scheme, this has lead to a very bad situation that even when any body other than the teacher makes a mistake the teacher is held responsible.

Conclusions

In general theoretically, the internal assessment scheme is the best as it leads to better understanding, better interaction and transparency in the system. However in practice it has certain lacuna arising out of the human and social behavior. However, with all the problems that exist, a continuous evaluation is certainly a better process.

9

CONDUCTING INTERNAL ASSESSMENTS

Dr. C. D. Lakkannavar
Professor and Head, Dept. of Chemistry,
S.D.M. College of Engg. & Technology,
Dharwad – 580 002

ABSTRACT

Getting passing marks 15 out of 25 in internal assessments (IAs) is a difficult task for academically weak students. This paper explains about the different guidelines to be followed in order to improve the performance of students in IAs remarkably and to facilitate the uniform and transparent conduction as well as evaluation of IAs.

Introduction

Conduction of internal assessments (IAs) in professional courses is highly essential to get the knowledge of the subjects phase wise, compel the students to study in advance and to score more in the university examinations. Uniform evaluation of internal assessments is highly essential, especially more in the wake of faculty members joining freshly.

Conduction of Internal Assessments

To facilitate the systematic conduction and evaluation of internal assessments, it is very essential to consider the following points:

- From the day of commencement of theory classes,

it is necessary to inform the students about the importance and conduction of the internal assessments.

- Faculty should have a clear concept of the blowups of all chapters.
- After covering the definite portion of the syllabus in every class, it is highly essential to discuss **all possible** questions on the portion covered with answers and ask the students to concentrate more on those questions.
- Give freedom to the students to raise their doubts and discuss on them.
- After covering the certain portion, a definite portion for IA should be given to the students well in advance at a minimum of week time.
- Set the question papers suitably for IA and questions should not be tough or easy. There shall be numerical problems without fail wherever they are essential. Check for all necessary data given in the problems and confirm about their solvability.
- Check for title of subject, examination, date of examination, duration of examination, marks allotted to the sub-questions, missing data, figure, clarity, grammar, ambiguity, syntax, etc.
- Scrutinize the question papers thoroughly by at least two faculty members or preferably by a departmental examination committee and finally they have to be approved by the head of the department.
- Strict confidentiality should be maintained in relation to the contents of question papers.
- Discuss thoroughly with the concerned faculty members about the scheme and solutions on the

question papers and get them prepared by the same faculty and finally they have to be approved by the head of the department.

- Scheme and solutions should be kept open for the students for their reference after the concerned IA.
- Answer papers should be valued referring scheme and solutions and the students are asked to go through the valuation. If the students quote any discrepancies about the valuation, concerned faculty must justify the marks given. If any mistake/s from faculty end, faculty has to accept without any hesitation and correct it without fail.
- This entire system should be continued for all the IAs and throughout the semester.

Conclusion

Transparent conduction and assessment of internal assessments will promote learning in a proper and desirable environment.

DISCUSSIONS

Q: The methods you explained are already followed here. However, there seems to be lot of reservation regarding this by the parents & students. Comment.

A: We have to convince the parents & students about VTU-rules and discipline what we have been maintaining by which we are making the students more alert towards studies and finally getting good placement.

Q: What are the rules and regulations for IA as set by VTU?

A: In simple, two IA's as normal procedure and third is for improvement. Questions should be of moderate complexity.

Q: Is it a good practice to give possible questions on each topic at professional college level?

A: There is nothing wrong in giving all possible questions in order to improve the performance of students. Please note that we are not giving those questions as important questions for IA.

10

EVALUATION THROUGH RATIONALISED GRADING SYSTEM

Dr. G. Neeraja Rani
Faculty, Dept. of Physics,
S.D.M. College of Engg. & Tech.,
Dharwad – 580 002

Dr. N.H. Ayachit
Prof. & HOD, Physics
S.D.M. College of Engg. & Tech.,
Dharwad- 580002

ABSTRACT

The true performance evaluation of a candidate in the examination system is a complex phenomenon. According to Hight, the scholarship must be accurate, however the difficult task involved in evaluating is interesting or other wise. This is because, this performance evaluation is going to decide the candidate's career in future. The evaluation at present is more dependent on the type of the question paper, the quality of the teacher involved in the teaching, his interest in transferring knowledge to the students and so on. Apart from all these, the grading of a candidate depends upon method of evaluation, i.e. the scheme and solutions for a given question paper, the general attitude of the teachers for evaluation and variation in evaluation at individual levels. These inherent properties of the system demand a rationalized methodology of evaluation and in this article, the grading system has been discussed as a tool towards improvising the system. This system, although not perfect, seems to be better for evaluation.

To start with, let us have some of the statements which throw light on the need of examinations.

Scholarship should be accurate whether it is interesting or not. **Hight**

The University evaluations are to be Universal/Global/ National/State/Institution Levels. **Bloom**

The evaluation process is to be such that it should eliminate all excessive elements of choice and subjectivity.

POA 1992

A basic source of misunderstanding which surrounds evaluation of a student lies in the fact that normally such evaluation has the vital consequences for one being evaluated, whereas it has no consequences for the one who does the evaluating. The grade student receives not only determine whether he graduates with honors or out of a School/College; they may also grade him in choosing his field of specialization, affects his plans of future and ultimately influence his carrier. On the other hand the grades a teacher gives do not affect his professional career, his commitment to a field of study or his future success as a scholar. A student may for a long time harbor a deep resentment against a teacher who grades him honestly, but were he to confront that teacher years later, the teacher might not even remember the student and would almost surely not remember the guide. Indeed, the teacher would most probably be astounded to learn the student cared so deeply about the grade. **Chon**

The above statements is true not only for a teacher but also for the University. The University system which has more than 10,000 teachers, as that in the case of VTU, if a trend and a feeling of this type develop, then the whole of the system would collapse. All of the above statements in general show the importance of requirement of fair examination system and process of grading. As we have to have a process of feeling only through the obstacles, so also the feel of our studies can be had through examinations. The better the obstacle, the better is the learning process. Thus, it is expected that the process of examinations has to be regular, up to a standard, such that the true performance of a candidate is projected in the form of a examination. The examinations have to come as milestones, which candidate not only remembers but also shows as his/her milestones of achievement to others. *Suppose you wanted to know a track of country , the worst way to do it would be to jump into a car, drive straight from one end to the other, and then turn back on it and walk away. How much better would you learn the country if before setting out, you were briefed and given maps to study; if you were to restart after proper re-orientation and questioning.*

<u>For most students and many teachers examination and grading are an unpleasant and unavoidable reality</u> *says Joseph Lauman. He further says that all students are concerned about exam and grades. Independent and capable to look forward to the challenge and potential success they offer are to be measured from our examination system. Being evaluated, represents, for most students a mixture of anxiety and positive anticipation.* Examination like athletic contests or artistic competition has to satisfy the needs of the students. Thus, it is essential that the examinations have to be such that it develops competitiveness ignoring individual differences in ability and temperament, but has to strike a balance between student needs to feel secure and face challenges. Thus, the examination system has to be such that it should not produce stress but reassure students as their true measure of performance. The examination system has been compounded with certain myths also, such as, the quantity of education that students receive is comparable with difficulty of earning high marks; grading with strictness will put teachers in the list of unpopularity among students; teachers think that to motivate the students evaluation has to be strict; some think that evaluation being strict encourages memorization and so on.

In any examination system two important aspects are observed; one is objective reform and the other is the behavioral aspect of examinations and the persons involved in the process.

It is not wrong to believe that any system would work, should all the persons involved in it attribute sincerity and skill, expected of them. In view of all the above mentioned facts the management of examination at a University level is of utmost importance. *Evaluation is an integral part of teaching learning process and so also is administration of the examination. A proper administration of examination system gives a feedback which is proper and hence enriches the teaching learning process.*

The examination process will yield,

- grading and certifying student
- Provides feed back to students and teachers
- Assisting in getting admission to various courses / progression outlets, including getting jobs (however, the people who matter in all these at present are not relying on examinations of University / Boards; they are conducting their own examinations).

If the examination serves such important functions, then it must be reliable and valid in assessing mental strengths, skills and values. To have scholarship accurate, assessment has to be rationalized in all respects. In a competitive world of today, it is very difficult to assess the performance of two persons and that of two groups. It is indeed a complex issue as far as assessment, generally in education field and especially in technical education, as the complexity arises due to various factors. One of the factors being, the nature of subjects differ especially when it comes to the choice of electives which are opted with an intension of providing insight into various types of developments taking place.

The performance in two subjects from the same students may differ depending on the nature of the subject like the advancement in the subject, the importance of the subject and so on. In case of choice of electives, the approach of students depend upon the attitude, possibility of passing without much difficulty, probability of scoring high marks and eagerness to learn the subject although the course is tough and so on. This approach of students may arise out of their ability in understanding earlier performance, guidance of others or his/her eye on the rank of the University. Although in the recent past the attitude of industry is getting changed toward the performance evaluation, still the university examination results are used as a major benchmark in evaluation of the performance of students. Acharya Ramamurthy committee set up in 1990 by the UGC reviewed the examination system of the Universities in India. Some of the points raised by it are:

- Examinations measure mainly rote memory
- Mainly essay type questions are used in the examination with 100% option.
- Evaluation is used for only grading and certification and not for instructional purposes.
- The performance in the results are not true measure of the ability of the student.

Of the above, the first two points lead to the next two points. As far as technical education is concerned, the first two points may not be that appropriate as far as rote memory and essay type questions are concerned, as the content of a question paper is determined by the curriculum. However, it is true that most of the faculty involved in question paper setting, try to see that the question papers are strictly in accordance with the first two points! Thus, the first two observations of the committee clearly indicate that the performance mainly depends upon the nature of the subject and the type of the question paper. This indeed, to a large extent, is true in engineering curricula, especially when it comes to the choice of electives. The curriculum of the Visveswaraiah Technological University, involves subjects coming under same group of electives like Biomedical Engineering (under Elective A), Reliability Engineering (under Elective B): TV Engineering (under Elective A), Neural Networks and Fuzzy System (under Elective B); Professional Communication (under Elective A), Graph Theory (under Elective B) and so on in the branch of Electronics & Communication Engg. The electives A and B belong to the same group and to the same semester such that only one elective in a group has to be selected. All subjects are mathematical are problem oriented. Naturally the performance in one subject will be different from the other even when the same student attempts.

The evaluation at present is more dependent on the type of the question paper, the quality of the teacher involved in the teaching, his interest in transferring knowledge to the students and so on. Apart from all these, the grading of a candidate depends upon methods of evaluation, i.e. the scheme and solutions for a given question paper, the general attitude of the teachers for evaluation in general and variation in evaluation at individual levels. These inherent properties of the system demand a rationalized methodology of evaluation and in this article, the grading system has been discussed as a tool towards improvising the system. This system although not perfect seems to be better for evaluation. In a rationalized system we need to calculate the root mean square value and fix the value such that it is at 50 and vary the proportional marks (1). However, this system is not with problems.

One can say most of our problems with evaluation will not exist if only two teachers exist as mentioned below as per Axelord.

"We have classified teachers' prototypes in two major categories. The first includes those teaching modes in which inquiry on the part of the student is not required or encouraged for the successful completion of the learning set by the professors. We call these teaching styles the didactic modes. The other category includes the teaching modes in which inquiry on the part of the student is required, if he is to complete successfully the tasks set by the teacher. We call these teaching styles as evocative modes. Those teachers who achieve excellence in didactic modes we shall call them as craftsmen; those teachers who achieve excellence in evocation modes shall be called artists".

REFERENCE

1. Proceedings of UGC Golden Jubilee National Seminar 2003 on Examination reforms, September, 11-13, 2003. M. S. University of Baroda, India.

11

PAPER SETTING STANDARDS

Dr. C.D. Lakkannavar
Professor and Head, Dept. of Chemistry
S.D.M. College of Engg. & Tech.,
Dharwad – 580 002

ABSTRACT

The placement of students in challenging organizations is highly dependent upon the academic ranking. The standard question papers are playing their own role in academic excellence. This paper discusses about the different points to be considered while setting the standard question papers.

Introduction

Setting a standard question paper is a challenging task of the examination system. Questions should be comprehensive, unambiguous and equitable to the students. Questions should evoke an analytical response from the students rather than a simple iteration of facts.

Standards of Paper Setting

To facilitate the setting of standard question papers, following points are to be carefully considered.

- The perfect blow ups of all the chapters referring the University prescribed books have to be taken into account.
- Paper setter should have a clear concept of the

blow ups of all the chapters.

- Then, set the questions covering the entire syllabus with almost all equal weightage on all the chapters.
- Questions should not be either tough or easy and there shall be numerical problems without fail wherever they are essential. Check for all necessary data given in the problem and confirm about their solvability.
- Questions should be set in such a way that there should not be much repetition from the previous years' question papers.
- Scrutinize the question papers scrupulously for their completeness.
- Scheme and solutions on the set question papers must be prepared by the paper setter only, to ensure the questions about their appropriateness.
- Without fail, check for title of subject, subject code, examination, year of examination, duration of examination, marks allotted to the sub-questions, missing data, out of syllabus questions, figure, clarity, grammar, ambiguity, syntax, etc.
- Give clear instructions such as, number of questions to be attempted, compulsory questions, sections, choice of questions from sections, all questions carrying equal marks, issue of hand books, steam tables, mathematical tables, charts, etc.

Conclusion

Paper setter should have a clear concept of the blow ups of all chapters. He should justify himself about the standard of question papers by scrutinizing the papers scrupulously, for all the points and preparing scheme and solutions of the papers accurately.

DISCUSSIONS

Q: Prescribing a textbook with sub articles having no continuity poses a problem for setting question paper. How to tackle this?

A: Careful approach should be followed by considering the blowup of the prescribed syllabus while setting the paper.

Q: University cites websites in reference lists. How to take this into account for Question paper setting?

A: This aspect needs thorough study.

Q: Is it possible to do justice to "question paper setting" when some individuals are assigned responsibility of setting 6-7 question papers?

A: Yes, it's not possible to do justice. University should follow "one paper per person" method.

12

INTERNAL ASSESSMENT IN ENGINEERING EDUCATION—NEED FOR A REVIEW

H. Vijay Murthy
Asst. Professor, E&E Dept.,
S.D.M. College of Engg. & Tech.,
Dharwad – 580 002
Email: hv_murthy@rediffmail.com

ABSTRACT

"Internal assessment" in the semester system of technical education is a routine and continuous evaluation process of student throughout the academic calendar. (It is not the TEST conducted with all the confidentiality as every one has misunderstood). This sort of continuous evaluation helps and enables the student to face the University exams with all the preparations and confidence. The marks obtained by student in internal assessment will be a boost to his/her performance on a percentage basis. Human desire is always to get more and more. Given an opportunity and congenial atmosphere, one always tries to better his/her earlier performance. In the highly polluted world of today, it is the bound duty of every educational institute and teacher to provide equal opportunity and congenial atmosphere to every student and involve and induce him /her to undergo continuous internal evaluation. By introducing the aspect of humanism here, it is possible to take the younger generation in right directions.

Preamble

In the yearly system of technical education, teaching was carried out in first nine months and student was expected to prepare for exams after that. The seriousness with which both teacher and student involve in curricular activity was comparatively less. Recollecting the subject taught long back and transforming it into an answer was difficult for the student. The percentage of success in first attempt was very poor due to (1) voluminous syllabi, (ii) poor student-teacher interaction, (iii) diversion of student's mind due to long gap and (iv) fear for exams.

Having understood the drawbacks of the yearly system of technical education, the Universities have adopted the semester system in which an year is divided into two parts, the entire syllabi of a course grouped into many small subjects and five to six subjects along with two practical sessions kept as contents of study for a semester. The exams are conducted twice in a year. This sort of piecewise segmentation of the whole course work was planned to make the students to regularly and continuously involve in their curricular development.

Significance of Internal Assessment

In semester system, ***internal assessment*** concept in its true spirits was introduced to make both the teacher and the student to continuously involve in academics. This means every semester teacher introduces a new subject in the student's mind, for about 15 to 20 hours, motivate the student to read, grasp and write. By giving appropriate assignments on the syllabus covered, teacher has to train the student to develop learning skills and reproducing capability. Finally, giving some task, all the above activities will have to be evaluated. To develop seriousness in the whole process, marks were introduced, that also help the student to better his/her performance in the final exams. Commitment, involvement and dedication from both the tutor and the taught is very much important here for the success of inculcating continuous learning habits.

It seems the concept is totally forgotten now. Internal assessment has been reduced to mere conducting TESTS with all the confidentiality (some colleges conduct IA tests like UPSC exams, valuing and awarding marks, no matter who gets how much), some other colleges conduct tests liberally. In both cases, shear negligence of teacher and the student have resulted in spoiling the importance of internal assessment. With a specific logic setup in the final exams for passing, many students gamble for success. From students point of view, this tendency may be due to lack of seriousness, preparedness, confidence, fear for exams & teachers. Lack of commitment, dedication and devotion from the teachers side, have further aggravated the situation. Added to this, now-a-days, various human factors viz., the likes & dislikes, sex discrimination, biasing, corruption, bossism, casteism etc., also play a very major role in the assessment process. In spite of the University guidelines, yardstick in the internal evaluation differs from individual to individual, department to department & college to college. Instances and experiences of the past, prove the vital role of human factor in the award of internal assessment marks.

Because the evaluation here is internal, having one to one relationship between the tutor and the taught, there exists a need to remove human factors stated above from the evaluation process. The setup should be transparent with the teacher committed to bring his/her students to the main stream of teaching-learning process through proper counseling. Every student must be assured of minimum required marks kept for internal assessment evaluation with he/she carrying out the assigned tasks given by the teacher with utmost sincerity. Gradation of students has to be done between minimum and maximum marks instead of between zero and maximum. Every teacher must commit to train students to this expectation.

Present Scenario

Earlier the University result itself was the final qualifying index for an individual to get job in Government or semi-Government sectors, private sector being very small in numbers. There was no much competition in the business world also. Each category of business being carried out by two or three companies who had better understandings and boundaries between them. There were no other selection procedures apart from University qualifying index, except in few cases thorough scrutiny was very much essential. Today in the highly competitive private business environment, each organization / industry insists on work efficiency, sharpness, behaviour, temperament, dynamism, competence, fitness etc., in a particular work to which the candidates are appointed. Hence they conduct their own entry level tests before an interview and finally gives appointment. Therefore, University result has lost its importance as final qualifying index for a job. Rather, it is now only an eligibility index for a particular cadre of job.

There are autonomous institutions like NITs around us that have credit system for the evaluation of their students. They get the highest quality input. 99.99% of them pass out getting their degree after the course work. Deemed Universities are also following the same path! With privatization being the talk of the day, many more private autonomous Universities are coming to reality in near future. In such context, it is right for all Universities to change their perspectives. With University result becoming only the eligibility index for any student's future career, it is the right time to think of sending the input, out after completing the course duration with proper gradation in their respective field of specialization.

Visveswaraiah Technical University is spread in the entire state in its geographical coverage. It is admitting students of PU level with 100% to 35% and with CET ranking from one to 60,000. With the ambition of all parents with 2+2 family structure to make their wards a professional graduate irrespective of their kids IQ level at any cost, has led the engineering students to undergo a lot of pressure. Many candidates with lower percentage and ranking get admitted by force, to the courses of not their choice. The University is offering around 20 specialized courses along with the three basic courses (Civil, Mechanical & Electrical). There are many instances of students not qualifying in subjects that were not at all required for their field of specialization. Due to the shortage of IA marks in these subjects, students are repeatedly failing and can not keep their terms. Since there is no provision for improvement of IA marks in the present rules, these students will be lagging in their education.

Humanism Aspects in Internal Assessment

Having accepted the students of below average to the professional course (35% compared to earlier 50% eligibility), expecting the same level of performance is not justified. Applying the same yardstick on these widely varied IQ level intake has resulted in a lot of malpractices/wrong practices in the evaluation system foregoing the basic ethics of examinations. It is observed that, aggrieved students and even their parents are making all possible out of way avenues for the success. Before VTU, technical education was through the other recognized Universities of Karnataka. They have wound up their courses after VTU was established. Studies and interviews conducted on the Karnataka University failed students reveal very harsh conclusions. Students admitted during 1980s & 1990s are not clearing subjects for want of IA marks. About 1000 students are still appearing for more than 10 subjects each, even after 10 to 15 attempts. Many have turned out to be criminals and many are psychic and are deprived of a better future.

'Survival of the fittest' is the law of nature. Live and let live is humanism. No mechanism on the earth should deprive an individual's right to grow, is the theme of humanism. More than 60% engineering graduates do not practice in the area of their specialization. Hard realities in the society are (i) a graduate of mechanical engineering working as an officer, in a housing finance, (ii) an electrical engineering graduate becoming a flutist, (iii) a computer graduate running a sweet stall and etc! Anything and everything is possible in an individual's life at any juncture. With all these possible, there is nothing wrong in allowing the input of the University out after course duration with a degree, without diluting the set standards.

This does not mean the standard should be lowered and sanctity of exams foregone. It only means to take teaching-learning process in its right spirits by all involved in it. The need has really come now to have a review into internal assessment guidelines of the University. To keep pace with the competing institutions it is high time that the University modify its IA guidelines and adopt humanistic vision, with proper and continuous monitoring the whole process.

Suggested Method

The following guidelines for internal assessment evaluation are suggested:

1. Assignments weighing 25 marks be given at the end of every 6 hours of teaching in each subject. The questions should be of University standard.
2. In 18 hours of teaching, three such assignments should be completed.
3. At the end of 20th hour, a one hour IA test of 25

marks weightage, comprising of a mixture of questions appearing in the above three assignments be conducted.

4. The evaluation of answer sheets should be carried out in the presence of respective students. The students have to be counseled then and there itself for their poor performance. Some more assignments may be given to them if the teacher feels necessary, to improve students performance.
5. Above steps are repeated at the end of 40th hour also.
6. For students who miss the tests on valid reasons as specified by the University, separate IA tests may be given on convenient dates.
7. Average of the above two IA tests will be the final marks awarded for the students. Minimum 60% should be assured for every student.
8. Every teacher should take up the responsibility in its true spirits for the success of the program. The departmental heads should monitor the proceedings at the department level and the dean academic at the college level. A methodology may be sorted out by the University to depute its representatives as and when required for an overall inspection. Penalty may be introduced.
9. All assignment and test papers have to be preserved with teachers till the end of term and have to be handed over to the students after recording the marks.

Based on the same analogy a method can be evolved to eliminate failures in practical exams that also involves human factors. All the above preparations done systematically, the student can face final theory exams with full confidence.

Minimum for passing at theory exams may be raised to 40%. Coded evaluation of answer books is to be continued to eliminate human factor.

Advantages of the Suggested Method

1. All students can be induced to reading, writing & learning process, without exam phobia.
2. The fear of failing in exams due to the shortage of IA marks will vanish and relieve the student from tension.
3. Involvement of huge man power to conduct IA exam can be minimized.
4. Victimization of students for various reasons stated earlier can be eliminated.
5. Faculty can be relieved from III IA evaluation work. This relief can be better utilized for any good cause.
6. Results of individual and university improve.
7. Human factor in IA evaluation can be eliminated to a great extent.
8. Students interaction in the subjects of their study increases as even an average or below average student definitely searches books or consults an intelligent student for correct answers for the given question.
9. Problem of preserving the IA books till the declaration of final results can be overcome by handing over the IA sheets to the students and asking them to preserve themselves.
10. The IA sheets with minimum 60% answers in them will definitely help the students while preparing for final exams.
11. As minimum is assured, many complications and legalities can be avoided.

12. A lot of unused papers, which would have gone as waste in IA books can be saved.

Conclusion

More than 30% of the students joining engineering are going away from the main stream of the society today. The reasons for this are mainly (i) non-orientation of tender minds during initial stages, (ii) ambition of parents to make their wards an engineer irrespective of their ward's capabilities (iii) student's fear for exams and teachers, (iv) irrelevant subjects (v) human factors, and (vi) no proper counseling are the reasons for this. Looking at all these factors, a method is suggested to bring those students to the main stream. A good student needs less care and a dull student more care. The factor of humanism is stressed here for better results.

ACKNOWLEDGEMENT

Author wishes to thank the authorities of SDMCET, Dharwad for providing all the encouragements and facility to prepare and publish this paper.

DISCUSSIONS

Q: There seems to be contradiction – sometimes you mention about humanity to be there and sometimes not – comment.

A: We should be human in our approach. Give routine assignments and IA to students. Conduct IA tests, setting questions from these assignment questions. In finalizing IA marks add weightage for assignments wherever minimum is to be assured. We should not disqualify any student admitted to course.

Q: Conducting more assignments – is it possible in our busy schedule?

A: We should do the primary duty more sincerely.

Q: Can we give marks for assignments – is it authorized?

A: My proposal is to be made to VTU for changing guidelines of IA.

Q: What's to be the pattern for IA paper – 8 or 5 questions?

A: Q.P. pattern is not relevant in my proposal. My view is- subject based pattern to be evolved by VTU thro' discussions.

Q: You propose to give 15 marks to the students. But is it not that they should take it?

A: I propose to train the students to get minimum marks. No teacher should award marks without stuff.

OTHER IMPRESSIONS

- Students are to be prepared to score marks.
- Wrong attitudes of faculty are the major cause of problems in IA related aspects.

13

ABOUT DEVELOPING QUESTION BANK

Dr. S. S. Bhavikatti
Professor & Head, Civil Dept. and Dean (Academic)
S.D.M. College of Engg. & Tech.,
Dharwad – 580 002

ABSTRACT

The author explains the concept of question bank system, which should not be a dead account. The author has open mind about the system. After explaining the merits and demerits of the system, the subject is opened for discussion. A suggestion is made and other suggestions are invited to find out whether it can be improved and implemented.

Introduction

The present day system of assessing the ability of a student to become an engineer is based on valuing his answers to few questions answered in specified time and on specified syllabus. Since the sincerity of each and every one is not believed, every individual/institution is not given powers to grade the students. The system of affiliating the institutions to universities has come into existence. Though the system is questioned often, no alternate acceptable system has been proposed so for. In this system of evaluation, whether there should be specified standard questions on which a student should be examined. Author discusses his concept of question bank, and the merits and demerits of creating question banks.

The Question Bank

A set of standard questions prepared by subject experts and approved by appropriate bodies in the university shall constitute the deposits in the question bank. The question shall be on the prescribed syllabus and to the required depth. The question bank account opened should not be a dead account. The interested teachers and paper setters should keep on contributing questions to the account. Depending upon the credit in the account, question paper setters should be instructed to draw only certain percentage of questions for the paper. To start with this percentage may be less and as the account builds up even up to 80-85 percent questions may be from this account. However, at no stage 100 percent questions are to be from the question bank alone. This forces paper setters to contribute new questions.

Merits of Question Bank System

There is good number of merits in having question bank system.

1. Some students, though they know the answers, they fail to understand the questions and often end with answers where they should have started. This happens particularity in descriptive subjects. If the question bank is made available to them, such mistakes may be eliminated.
2. Students try to find answers for all thc questions in the question bank and in the process acquire good knowledge.
3. In the affiliated colleges system, some students get added advantage due to question appearing in the format they are trained. This situation is particularly so, in the advanced topics where there is no standard text books which covers entire syllabus.

4. Often missing data in question papers perturbs the students in the examinations. This situation can be avoided if proper question bank is developed.

Demerits of the System

As in any other system, this system has also got a certain demerits which are listed below:

1. Guide books will start appearing in the markets which will concentrate answering the questions, rather than explaining the subjects.
2. During the examinations some students may get tempted to smuggle answers which are readily available outside.

Conclusions

Any system is having merits and demerits. It is necessary to weigh them and decide whether to accept the system. The topic is opened for the discussion in the workshop. It may be discussed, whether the demerits can be plugged by suitably modifying the system. One method of doing so may be making our question compulsory which is not in the question bank. The deciding factor shall be ultimately based on whether it makes students to learn the subject properly and helps us in assessing his ability to learn the subject.

DISCUSSIONS

Q: For whose reference is the question bank – students or staff?

A: For the reference of both staff and students. Question bank is to make the questions clear to the students. Question paper setter can also refer to it. Some percent of questions can be taken directly from the question bank.

Q: For the programming subjects, there cannot be limited set of questions. How to develop question bank for such subjects?

A: Questions can be simply added without violating the syllabus.

Q: Will it not kill the creativity of the students?

A: No. There is no need to check creativity in regular subjects. Here the aim is to give maximum information about well-developed subjects within the time allotted. Students' ability to answer should be checked not by his ability to understand questions. Seminars and project works are meant for developing creativity not the regular subjects.

Q: What is your opinion regarding diluting quality of the question papers?

A: It's not the quality of questions, instead, the pattern is diluting.

Q: As experienced in an earlier attempt, after few years, question bank gets saturated. This results in habit of only memorizing and not thinking.

A: It is good that the students are at least memorizing. In the process they understand the subject to great extent.

Q: Theory questions can be put in different words. But what about the problems?

A: Data can be changed; parameter to be determined can be changed.

Comments: Staff members can think of bringing out question bank starting from I Sem. Because our college is not autonomous college, the question bank can be used in Internal Assessment test.

14

TIPS FOR COMPITITIVE EXAMINATIONS FOR ENGINEERING GRADUATES

Shiralashetti S.C.
Faculty, Dept. of Mathematics,
S.D.M. College of Engg. and Tech.,
Dharwad-580 002.

ABSTRACT

Engineering graduates are aware of various competitive examinations conducted thought out the year in our country. The purpose of this article is to create awareness about the examinations, their schedules, methods of preparations, strategies to be adopted. Believing in an idea and implementing it is often the key to success. Being communicative with commitment and creativity, could lend an upper edge in today's highly competitive job market.

Keywords: Competitive Exams, study hours, concentration, Meditation, consistency, selectivity & reflective study etc.

1. Introduction

Candidates appearing at competitive examination would be facing an examination, which in many aspects differs from the university type exam. Consequently, the technique of preparation has to be different to suit the matrix of this examination. There is a lot of teaching in our universities but very little learning takes place because of a general air of indifference and intellectual inertia which show lack of training in focusing the mental potential, on the part of the students as well as teachers. Every student does possess an overload of worries, fears, hopes and anxieties but one must learn to minimize these factors during the preparations and at the time of exam. To be cool is a fashion these days but we are rarely able to achieve that type of mental state since the anxieties still manage to get into our way. So most of the time it is you who is getting into your own way. Thus it is you who will have to clear out of your way. Only when you are clam and collected you can read and think fast. The student should develop through suitable techniques a mental architecture by using which he can easily hold and recall information in a fast and orderly manner.

But the way, it should be borne in mind that there is no element of chance in getting through competitive exam. **Remember Success is when Preparation Meets performance.** Further, also remember competition is nothing new to you. Darwin tells us that man is a survivor of many competitions that he had to face early in this career like most other animals or species. Hence, we are all born with a strong survival instinct and ability to compete well for most of our needs. The situation in civil services competition is no different.

The most effective tool that you have got to win in this competition is your brain which is like a sleeping giant. Recent researches in psychology, education, genetics, physics, and mathematics have shown that the potential of your brain is for greater than was generally imagined. Even the earlier statement that on average we use only one percent of our brains may be well be wrong because it now seems that we use even less than one percent- which means that an enormous amount of your mental capability is never used by you. As you very well know today's society is a knowledge driven society. So your mind is the most important tool in this knowledge- based environment. Hence mind is man's ultimate weapon and I call upon you to use it with confidence for success in anything that you do.

Be fit in theory, committed in practice. And achieve the BEST

2. Competitive Examinations

2.1 Competitive Exams by UPSC.

1. Civil Service Examinations by UPSC
2. Engineering Service Examination conducted by UPSC.
3. Combined Defense Services Examination.
4. Permanent Commission in the Army Technical Graduates Course.
5. Permanent /Short Service Commission in Education Branch of the Indian Navy.
6. Commissioned Officer in Education, Law and Logistic Branches in Indian Navy.
7. Air Traffic Control Cords and Education engineering and Electrical Indian Navy.
8. Women Pilots in Short Service Commission.
9. Women Pilot Trainees in Air Force.
10. Naval Armament Inspection Officer in Indian Navy.
11. Short Service Commission in the Electrical or Engineering branch in the Indian Navy.
12. Asst. Commandant (Technical) in Cost Guard.
13. Aeronautical Engineers Course in the IAF.
14. Permanent Commission Course/ SSC Course for Electronics and Mechanical Branch in Air Force.
15. Short Service Commission for Technical Branch.
16. Male officers in permanent Commission/ Male and Female officers in SSC (Technical Branch).

17. Technical Graduates Course and Short Service Commission (Technical).

18. University Entry Scheme for permanent Commission in the Army.

2.2. Competitive Exams by State Public Service Commission.

1. Bihar Public Service Commission.
2. Gujarat Public Services Commission.
3. Haryana Public Service Commission.
4. Himachal Pradesh Public Service Commission.
5. Karnataka Public Service Commission.
6. Madhya Pradesh Public Service Commission.
7. Maharshtra Public Service Commission.
8. Manipur Public Service Commission.
9. Nagaland Public Service Commission.
10. Orissa Public Service Commission.
11. Uttar Pradesh Public Service Commissionm, etc.

3. Tips on How to Prepare for Competitive Examinations

1. General: One of the top secrets of Success in Competitive Examination is that most of the toppers concentrate on their study without time and again thinking of getting into the top ranks. That is why when the results come. They are often surprised and generally reveal that they hardly thought they would come up with such brilliant success. It does not mean that they were not hopeful or confident. They were and they did strive hard to achieve the best on the other hand, there are students. Who do little to achieve the desired goal. Day dreaming and wishful thinking can hardly lead to success. At the same time, concentrating too much on the negative aspect of your results is bound to affect your performance. Psychologically, you should have a very positive and confident approach while preparing for the competitive examinations. Besides this, to be a successful administrator, after your dream to join an administrative service is realized, you should prepare your self by developing the qualities of leadership, keen observation, trouble shooting. Crisis is management, patience to listen to others, good communication skills, ability to speak effectively and with clarity, cheerful personality and objectivity in your thoughts and actions.

2. **When to Begin:** The right time to start preparing for Competitive Examinations is from the school stage itself because the UPSC and KPSC expect the candidates to have cumulative knowledge. Later preparations cannot compensate on this account. For example, at the school stage if you have studied calculus it will be helpful in enriching your analytical powers. Besides, one also needs to develop the power of comprehension and assimilation for which one can prepare right from the senior classes of school.

3. **Study Hours:** It is interesting to know that toppers are not born to top but they are also students like you. But they reached the top because they did stick to their study programs without postponing it even for a day. You need not study ate war level (which may result in stress) but a study of 10 to 12 hours a day right from the beginning will suffice. If you are making your preparation right form the graduation level, study of five to six hours is adequate, continuous study stretching over too long hours at one go may not prove as useful as studying with little breaks in every two to three hours but regularity is a must.

4. **Study Schedule:** Time is perhaps one of the most crucial factors for preparation of competitive Examinations. You may plan a time table for each day to cover your subjects.

You have to devote as much time as you feel necessary to achieve your goal. Whatever time schedule you fix up, you must add here to it in a disciplined manner. There is liberally no substitute to regular study.

You must be devoted whole heatedly and determined to clear this examination. Taking it lightly or preparing for some other examinations, along with studying for the competitive examination has not helped most of the students applying this approach.

5. **Proper Planning:** A big unity is attached to planning. Plan your studies properly with due regard to your strengths and weaknesses i.e. identify your strong and weak areas. Clearly, you must know in which subject you have a strong base and which are the areas where you need to study more. Good planning really implies maximum results with the minimum of efforts. And effective planning means that you work out your own mechanism for checking whether you are spending your own time effectively or not. To be really effective and useful all the study and learning must be finished well before the examination.

6. **No Substitute to Hard Work:** There are no prescriptions for guaranteed success in exams. However, you should be ready to put in hard lab our, if experience of a CSE topper is any guide, "Hard work, a devotion to the goal one has set for one self and systematic study can take you to your desired goal", Do less but do it thoroughly.

7. **Concentration**: concentration is absolutely essential for study and better performance in exams. The ability to connectable is partly a natural gift and partly a matter of training and practice. Congenial atmosphere for study is very necessary. An environment which is free from disturbance like a library is a good place for study. A good library providès you the right study environment, suitable company,

inspiration any even opportunities for discussion, beside useful reference material and books.

8. **Meditation:** Daily practice 15 to 20 Minutes Meditation, after noon before food. Meditation governs the affections, directs our actions, corrects excesses, softens the manners, adorns and regulates the life, and lastly bestows the knowledge of things divine and human alike.

9. **Gaining Confidence**: Don't have worries. Be enthusiastic and look ahead. Be optimistic. Repeat to yourself that you will make it to IAS. This will add to your confidence. Never doubt your potential because what a man has already done, a man can also do. Always remember dedication and determinations are necessary ingredients of success.

10. **Consistency**: consistency in your preparation is of vital importance. One usual mistake made by candidates is putting in extraordinarily long hours of preparation. Just a few days before the exam. In fact you should arrange your preparation in such a manner that as the examination draws nearer you should rather feel comfortable and relaxed both physically and mentally, especially on the examination days.

11. **Hard Decisions:** increase or decrease the hours that you devote to study depending on availability of your time. If necessary take hard decisions. Such as you may ignore topics which need less attention completely. Such decisions are not always desirable but they may be better than trying to study everything when you simply do not have the time.

12. **Evolve Your Own Method:** rely on your own method of study believing that this is the only right method. For example, if you like to study silently do accordingly. If you prefer a particular spot for your study it is better to sit there. Also, you may develop habit of reading fast. Reading rapidly will save your time.

13. Studying Together: study with a fellow or a group of friends who are also preparing for the same Exam. Regular discussions with such friends are very helpful. This way you not only revise what you have studied but also learn many points which you might not have covered or did not know. Such a company happens to be of supplementing nature to each other. Besides, it makes your study more interesting and competitive

14. Selective & Reflective Study: your study should be quality based not quantity based. You should not lay emphasis on just reading more and more books, magazines and journals but reflect on your subject and try to master it., you should develop you rational faculty to assimilate relevant information and analyze problems dispassionately. Your reading must be purposeful. Distinguishing between the important and the unimportant reading material you must keep in mind what is useful from the competitive examination point of view.

15. Coaching: Coaching by itself may prove helpful in making you regular in your preparation. It is also beneficial since it provides you an opportunity to interact and discuss your preparation strategy and your problems with your classmates and also with your professional teachers. In order to take full advantage of coaching you must revise regularly at home what ever you learn at the coaching institute. It is better if coaching is over at least a month before the examination so that you are left with sufficient time to make revisions and do practice.

16. Weekly Revision: you should keep one day in a week for revision work so that you could review the progress made and see what you have done and how much more or quicker pace is needed. Periodical analysis of what you have studied and its consolidation is necessary. It will make you realize your weakness and your strengths. Without this periodical stop-over you will keep on learning and you may forget what you piled up in your mind earlier.

17. Before Facing The Exam: start revision early and practice answering questions on the pattern of the examination fixing up the time and words limit. To gain confidence and learn to bear the pressure you are likely to face in the examination hall. This will give you an opportunity to know what type of difficulties you may encounter in the examination and to prepare yourself to meet such challenges.

18. Medical Standard: it is worth while to keep in mind the medical requirements especially in case one thinks of joining CDSE, IPS, RPF Group B police Services because all your efforts will go waste if ultimately you are denied service because of your failure to meet the prescribed medical standards.

19. Interview: The interview or the personality test is the last stage before being selected in the civil services. The requirement of appearing in the interview is to qualify the main examination. Generally, the ratio between interviewed conditions and the selected ones is 2:1. There is a lot of hype about the interview and the Myths need to be punctured; it is not just a list of your knowledge. Personality test, as the name suggests, assesses the personality of a candidate. Personality attributes or includes leadership qualities, the ability to tackle difficult problems, the ability to withstand pressure, the interest in the extra- curricular activities. The interpersonal abilities or presentation skills are listed here rather than the depth of information.

20. Success Through Positive Thinking: It is easy in the world to live after the world opinion; it is easy in solitude to live after ones own opinion; but the great man is he who in the midst of the crowd keeps with perfect sweetness the independence of solitude.

REFERENCES

1. Hand Book for competitive Examination by L. Raghvendra.
2. Advance General Studies for Competitive Examination by .S. Kumar.
3. Engineering Services Examination by S. G. Gupta.
4. Combined Defense services Examination by S.P. Sharma.
5. Career options for Engineering Graduates: by Neelam Soni. "SAP".

THEME C

RESEARCH AND TECHNICAL WRITING

15

RESEARCH NEED AND OPPORTUNITIES

Dr. V. S. Hegde
Assistant Professor, Dept. of Civil Engg.,
S.D.M. College of Engg. and Tech.,
Dharwad- 580002

ABSTRACT

Research is part of teaching activities in higher education. Classroom teaching is expected to develop thinking process in the mind of students. Research experiences help teacher to motivate students and train them to develop innovative thinking, which is the essence of education. More than the facility, attitude of research is very important for effective research. Realizing this need, there are a large number of agencies supporting research activities. Some of the important funding agencies are UGC, DST, CSIR, AICTE, DOD, ISRO, DOE, DRDO, MOWR, PRL, etc. Well-drafted proposals are considered for grants from the agencies. A well defined problem with clear objectives achievable in the given time period, appropriate methodology, clear knowledge of state of art, outcome of the research work and properly justified budget are some of the characteristics of good proposal.

Introduction

Classroom teaching is aimed to motivate students and develop for innovative thinking process and train them and develop this attitude. It is believed that research experience of the teacher help him to discharge this task effectively. Because of research activities, teacher develops innovative thinking, attitude of inquiry mind, and get training in this direction. His experience gained in his research endeavor like analyses of facts and logical arguments, constraints, and inferences can be imparted at teaching level. Therefore, research is considered as part of teaching activities at higher education level.

Infrastructure and Opportunities

Although research at advanced level needs lot of infrastructure, in the beginning it is not the major components. Research needs attitude of inquiry, which is a mental status. This attitude is to be developed and cultivated. Further, in the initial stages, infrastructure cost is not high and is affordable even at individual level. However, at advanced level, it needs lot of input, which an individual cannot afford. These research input has a lot impact on out quality of teaching, quality of out put, and national economic scenario. Realizing this need, a lot of agencies are coming forward to support research activities in the country. Some of the important agencies are UGC, DST, Dept of Ocean Devt., ISRO, PRL, CSIR, MHRD, AICTE, KSCST, DRDO, DOE, UNESCO and so on. Apart from these many bilateral exchange programs, Industries are also available.

Each agency has set of objectives and mission and our research interest is complimenting their mission our proposals stand high. Every year, these agencies bring out a booklet containing the thrust areas of research. There may be little difference in their format. But in common, a good proposal has

1. Clearly stated problem, model based–conceptual or mathematical; analytical, experimental etc, application and merits of the model,
2. Definition and scope of the problem,

3. Status of art both at national level and international level, gap in the knowledge,
4. Objective and how this gap will be narrowed,
5. Approach in flow chart showing how different components of the work are interrelated and organized,
6. Detailed methodology of data acquisition and data analyses both laboratory, statistical, mathematical etc.,
7. Outcome of the research work/ beneficiaries
8. Implementation of work showing time schedule of work, out put based, deliverable product at the end of every year,
9. Budget,
10. Competence and expertise of the investigator to carryout the work.

Processing

The whole process from submission to implementation is nearly a year program. When proposal is received by the agencies it is verified and processed by the funding agencies (non technical) and sent to experts for evaluation. Proposal is rated as poor < 5 points are generally rejected; If points scored is 5-7, proposal is asked for revision and improvements and resubmission; and if points scored is >7, are called for personal presentation. During the personal presentation if experts committee is convinced about the scientific content and expertise of the investigator, it is recommended for grants. Then it is processed at account level and sent for approval.

The experts, while evaluation, generally consider the following points.

1. Clarity of Objective: Precise and well formulated; Fair; Vague and fussy.
2. Work plan and methodology: Appropriate; Not clear.
3. Expertise and competence authenticated by published work.
4. Validity of assumption and analyses.
5. Significance of the research and deliverable product.
6. Budget.

Presentation

A good presentation either starts with a social relevance of the outcome of the research work or its contribution to the knowledge. Then the scientific content, approach, model involved, and expertise, collaboration involved and budget required. All interaction with experts in a high academic spirit and positive mood is the added advantage.

Conclusion

Submission of proposal and getting grants is like a game. Some times a good proposal also fails because of tough competition. Therefore a positive attitude both for submission and research is a must. We must enjoy research and it should be a way of life and mental attitude.

16

WRITING RESEARCH PAPERS

Rekha V. Dundur
Asst. Professor, Dept. of E&C,
S.D.M. College of Engg. & Tech.,
Dharwad- 580002

Dr. M.V. Latte
Asst. Professor, Dept. of E&C,
S.D.M. College of Engg & Tech.,
Dharwad- 580002

ABSTRACT

Writing a research article is an important parameter. The article should be presented in a methodological way such that, in short, it should represent the concepts and conclusion. In this article some of the salient features are presented as universally accepted and discussed.

Introduction

"A journey of a thousand miles is begun with a single step" goes a Chinese saying. Don't let the fear of the paper keep you from....

Getting Started

- The first thing to do is to allot enough time for the work. For an average length of (10-20 pgs) a month is required to adequately collect the library research and materials. A bare minimum is a week.

- It's very important to start research with a solid thesis statement. This is the question proposed to be answered in the paper. A couple of hints
    1. It should be simple, an enormous subject is not comfortable to work with.
    2. Make sure the idea will work. Preliminary research in the library is to be done to sure there is enough available material on the topic.
    3. Some time should be taken to familiarize with the libraries.

General Form of a Research Paper

An objective of organizing a research paper is to allow people to read the work selectively, where the interest may be in just the methods, a specific result, the interpretation, or just the summary of the paper to determine if it is relevant to the study, To this end, many journals require the following sections, submitted in the order listed, each section to start on a new page. There are variations of course, some journals call for a combined results and discussion, or include modules and methods after the body of the paper.

The paper is normally submitted in the following form and style

- Title page
- Abstract
- Introduction
- Modules and methods
- Results
- Discussion
- Literature Cited

To make a paper readable the following style could be used.

- Print or type using a 12-point standard font, such as Times, Geneva, Bookman, Helvetica etc.
- Text could be double spaced on 81/2"x11" paper with 1" margins, single sided.
- Number pages consecutively
- Start each new section on a new page.
- Adhere to recommended page limits

Mistakes to avoid

- Placing a heading at the bottom of a page with the following text on the next page.
- Dividing a table or figure- confine each figure/ table to a single page.
- Submitting a paper with pages out of order.

In all sections of the paper

- Stay focused on the research topic of the paper
- Use paragraphs to separate each important point (except for the Abstract)
- Present points in logical order.
- Use present tense to report well accepted facts.
- Use past tense to describe specific results.
- Avoid informal wording, addressing the reader directly, and jargon or slang terms.
- Avoid use of superfluous pictures-include only those figures necessary to presenting results.

(i) Title Page

Select an informative title. Include the name(s) and address(es) of all authors.

(ii) Abstract

The summary could be 200 words or less. An Abstract is a concise single paragraph summary of completed work or work in progress. In a minute or less a reader can learn the rationale behind the study, general approach to the problem, pertinent results, and important conclusions or new questions.

Writing an Abstract

The summary should be written after the rest of the paper is completed. Economy of words is important throughout any paper, but especially in an Abstract. However, use complete sentences and do not sacrifice readability for brevity. Summarize the study, including the following elements in any Abstract. Try to keep the first two items to no more than one sentence each.

- Purpose of the study-hypothesis, overall question, objective
- Model and brief description of the experiment.
- Results, including specific data- preferably quantitative if that is the form taken by the data, results of any statistical analysis should be reported.
- Important conclusions or questions that follow from the experiment(s).

Style

- Single paragraph and concise
- As a summary of work done, it is always written in past tense.
- An Abstract should stand on its own, and not refer to any other part of the paper such as a figure or a table.
- Focus on summarizing results - limit background information to a sentence or two, if absolutely necessary.

- What you report in an Abstract must be consistent with what you reported in the paper.
- Correct spelling, clarity of sentences and phrases, and proper reporting of quantities (proper units, significant figures) are just as important in an Abstract as they are anywhere else.

(iii) Introduction

Introductions should not exceed two pages (double spaced, typed). See the examples in the writing portfolio package.

The purpose of an introduction is to acquaint the reader with the rationale behind the work, with the intention of defending it. It places work in a theoretical context, and enables the reader to understand and appreciate objectives.

Writing an Introduction

The Abstract is the only text in a research paper to be written without using paragraphs in order to separate major points. Here is the minimum information that should be included in a successful introduction.

- Describe the importance (significance) of the study –why was this worth doing in the first place? Provide a broad context.
- Defend the model. A comment may be made on its suitability from a theoretical point of view as well as indicate practical reasons for using it.
- Provide a rationale. State your specific hypothesis(es) or objective(s),and describe the reasoning that lead you to select them.
- Very briefly describe the experimental design and how it will accomplish the stated objectives.

Style

- Use past tense except when referring to established facts. After all, the paper will be submitted after all of the work is completed.
- Organize your ideas, making one major point with each paragraph. If you make the four points listed above you will need a minimum of four paragraphs.
- Present background information only as needed in order support a position. The reader does not want to read everything about the subject.
- State the hypothesis or objective precisely- do not over simplify.
- As always, pay attention to spelling, clarity and appropriateness of sentences and phrases.

(iv) Modules and Methods

There is no specific page limit, but a key concept is to keep the section as concise as possible. Since this is read selectively. Modules and methods may be reported under separate subheadings within this section or can be incorporated together.

Writing a Modules and Methods Section

Modules

- Include specialized equipments or supply not commonly found in laboratories.
- Do not include commonly found supplies.
- If use of a specific type of equipment of a particular supplier is critical to the success of the experiment then it and the source should be singled out, otherwise no.
- Modules may be reported in a separate paragraph

or else they may be identified along with procedures.

Methods

- Methodology is to be reported (not details of each procedure that employed the same methodology).
- The methodology is described completely including specifics.
- To be concise, methods are to be presented under headings devoted to specific procedures or group of procedures.
- The methods should be generalized that is report how procedures were done, not how they were specifically performed on a particular day.
- If well-documented procedures were used, they are reported by name or reference.

Style

- Active voice which would focus the readers attention on the investigator rather than the work would be awkward. Therefore when writing up the methods most authors use third person active voice.
- Normal prose is to be used in this section and in every other section of the paper – informal lists should be avoided and complete sentences should be used.

What to Avoid

- Modules and methods are not a set of instructions.
- All explanatory information and background should be omitted and saved for the discussion.
- Information that is irrelevant to a third party should be omitted.

(v) Results

The page length of this section is set by the amount and types of data to be reported. Continue to be concise, using figures and tables, if appropriate, to present results most effectively.

The purpose of a result section is to present and illustrate findings. This section should be made a completely objective report of the results in all interpretation should be saved for the discussion.

Writing a Results Section

IMPORTANT: Material that would normally be included in a research article should be clearly distinguished from any raw data or other appendix material that would not be published. Such material should not be submitted unless requested by the instructor.

Content

- Summarize findings in text and illustrate them, if appropriate, with figures and tables.
- In text each result should be described, pointing the reader to observations that are most relevant.
- Results of control experiments should be described and observations that are not presented in a formal figure or table should be included, if appropriate.
- Data should be analyzed and then the analyzed data should be prepared in the form of a figure (graph), table or in the form of a text.

What to Avoid

- Do not discuss or interpret results, report background information, or attempt to explain anything.

- Never include raw data or intermediate calculations in a research paper.
- Do not present the same data more than once.
- Do not confuse figures and tables – there is a difference.

Style

- As always, use past tense when referring to results, and put everything in logical order.
- In text, refer to each figure as "figure 1", "figure2", etc.; number tables as well.
- Place figures and tables, properly numbered, in order at the end of the report (clearly distinguish them from any other material such as raw data, standard curves, etc.).
- Figures and tables may be placed within the text of the result section.

Figures and Tables

- Either place figures and tables within the text of the result, or include them in the back of the report (following Literature Cited).
- Figures and tables are placed at the end of the report. They should be clearly distinguished from any attached appendix materials, such as raw data.
- Regardless of placement, each figure must be numbered consecutively and complete with caption.
- Regardless of placement, each table must be numbered consecutively and complete with heading.

(vi) Discussion

Journal guidelines vary. The objective here is to provide

an interpretation of results and support all conclusions using evidence from experiment and generally accepted knowledge, if appropriate.

Writing a Discussion

Data should be interpreted in the discussion in appropriate depth. A phenomenon when explained must explain mechanisms also. If results differ from expectations, explain why that may have happened. If results agree, describe the theory that the evidence supported. It is never appropriate to simply state that the data agree with expectations, and let it drop at that.

- Decide if each hypothesis is supported, rejected, or if a decision cannot be made with confidence. Do not simply dismiss a part of study or a study as "inconclusive".
- Conclusion should be made and suggestions as to how the experiment should be modified, if necessary, in order to properly test the hypothesis(es) or accomplish the objectives.
- Explain all observations as much as possible, focusing on mechanisms.
- Decide if the experimental design adequately addressed the hypothesis, and whether or not it was properly controlled.
- Try to offer alternative explanations if reasonable alternatives exist.
- Be creative; do not be afraid to speculate. Individual report guidelines will provide suggestions.

Style

- When referring to information, distinguish data generated from studies from that of published information or from information obtained by others.

- Refer to work done by specific individuals in past tense.
- Refer to generally accepted facts and principles in present tense.

(vii) Literature Cited

- List all literature cited in the report in alphabetical order by first author or in the order of reference.
- If you are citing an on line journal use the journal citation (name, volume, year, page numbers).
- Some of the reports may not require references in that case state that "no references were consulted".

REFERENCE

1. www.ruf.rice.edu/reportform.html
2. Strunk, W. Jr. & White, E.B. The Elements of Style

DISCUSSIONS

Q: If the author selects for his paper a topic making sure that "idea is correct" – does it not mean there will be no scope for new thinking / research?

A: The intention behind telling this is that one should avoid impossible or wild imaginations. However it is not at the cost of creativity.

REMARKS

- There is difference between theoretical, analytical and experimental type paper writing.
- In a technical paper the references are given in the order of their occurrence. In a text book they are given in alphabetical order.

17

ART OF WRITING TECHNICAL PAPER USING AVAILABLE RAW INFORMATION

Dr. H.G. Gopal
Professor & Head, Dept. of E&E,
S.D.M College of Engg. & Tech.,
Dharwad- 580 002
Email : akshaygopal_hg@yahoo.co.in

Ramesh L. Chakrasali
Asst.Professor, Dept. of E&E,
S.D.M. College of Engg. & Tech.,
Dharwad- 580 002

ABSTRACT

In science and technology, experiments are designed and conducted to either prove or demonstrate a hypothesis. These experiments may be either analytical, semi analytical or purely experimental. In this process one gets lot of data. Lot of analyses, tests for correctness of data and presentation of data in final form is the basic task before preparing any write up. Drawing conclusions based upon the final presentable data will be the next task. A paper cannot be visualized in its final form in the beginning itself. Thus while writing a paper a systematic step by step procedure is to be followed so as to make the paper comprehensive, simple, lucid and meaningful. The objective of this paper is to propose a method to convert the available / generated / existing experimental raw data into a scientific or technical paper.

Introduction

Design of experiments to test either an existing hypothesis or a new one or questioning the authenticity of existing standard etc., is important in science and engineering. It may be either to verify a simple Ohm's law or finding Young's modulus of a material etc. Proper planning of experiment, clear cut vision about the data generated and its analyses to derive meaningful conclusions are vital for the success of any scientific investigation. Total involvement, dedication and commitment from the teacher or researcher towards the task are always of higher priority. In the field of engineering as more and more work is carried out, one gets mastery over the subject and makes him/her to think in diverse ways that will result in innovations, quick reflections, substantiation etc. For example in teaching profession, when teachers teach either a subject or conducts practical or guides some project/seminar or accompanies students to education tours will get more information about the subject under consideration. In this process, in many cases some idea about improving the existing system or doubts or justification for the existing some rules/hypothesis arises. In order to satisfy his/her curiosity, more work has to be done by the teacher giving emphasis on the factor(s) on hand. This will lead to further investigation, study, analysis, experimentation, discussion etc. Thereby making not only him/her, but also a small group of friends to think about the problem and work for ways of getting the solution. Based on success of the experiment(s), there is a need to place the results on paper in a concise form. This will further invoke discussions among larger learned class to fine tune the information.

Methodology

In the process of writing a paper, depending upon the problem on hand, many information need to be gathered to justify the analyses carried out on the data and finally to arrive at some conclusions. This demands a systematic approach. Before discussing the data analyses part, focus is given to the methods of getting the data. Data can be (1) existing or generated, (2) on line or offline, which strictly depends upon the problem on hand and the nature of analyses to be carried out.

Data can be obtained by any one of the following

1. Information can be had by literature survey (through reading, scanning, skimming etc.), by using both conventional and digital library facilities.
2. An experiment can be designed, conducted on a concept or hypothesis and the observed data are collected.
3. Analyses of some problem(s) may give surprising results that forms data for further investigation.
4. Based on some improvement in the existing analytical formulation, simulations can be carried out to generate further data.
5. Statistical data collection like weather forecasting, population, examination results, stock market happenings, referendums on some issues, economic or feasibility surveys generate lot of data.

Now it is the time to think and present the information in a comprehensive, simple, lucid and meaningful way by quoting appropriate theoretical background. There are many ways of analyzing the data for example one may prefer to use statistical methods to process the data and derive conclusions. In majority of the cases, more particularly for data obtained from experiments, graphs are drawn. Based on these graphs conclusions are drawn. In few cases analytical equations are formulated looking into the trends of these graphs. Results of the simulations obtained on the analytical formulation and experimental observations are compared in many cases, to propose a mathematical model.

Once the above task is completed the same is to be transferred on to the paper. To begin with one should not bother about the format, continuity, proficiency of the language etc., as it seriously affects ones original thinking. As and when thoughts arise the same is to be written. After putting down the entire thoughts on the paper, formatting has to be done considering continuity of thought, language, margins etc. The paper should have an objective and the write-up should be on this on this objective till the end.

The Style

While writing a technical/scientific paper, steps given below are generally followed

(a) Problem definition: Here a brief introduction to the problem giving emphasis on the existing situation, need for taking up the present investigation considering the lacunae or inconvenience in the present system or highlighting the relevance of the outcome of the present study are furnished.

(b) Literature survey: In this section, author gives the details of the existing status with proper citations in the order of reference in the text with his/her critical comments. In case of experimental investigations proper justifications are also given comparing the earlier one.

(c) Clear cut narration of the method by which data is obtained. For example,

   (i) Present work: Here the details of work envisaged are furnished with experimental/ simulation details, supporting photographs of experimental setup or waveforms obtained etc.

(ii) Standard followed or questioned while conducting the experiment(s).

(d) Data processing: It is quite important to analyze the data obtained from the investigation. One may prefer to use statistics, regression analyses, curve fitting techniques for his/her analyses and modeling or to arrive at meaningful results. It is necessary to present details of the technique adopted for data processing the data in the paper.

(e) Presentation of obtained/processed data: Outcome of the investigation is presented in a systematic way either through well planned tabulation or figures or graphs or charts, etc. If this is well planned, it minimizes majority of writing. However they must be presented with appropriate captions and proper citation in the text. IEEE and other standard journals prescribe caption to the figures should be at the bottom while caption to tables at the top.

(f) Results & Discussions: Here usually author puts his/her discussion for each result obtained in a critical way. Many times present results and published results in the literature are superimposed on graphs or tables for discussion purpose. While doing so one should not try to dilute the essence of the published work.

(g) Conclusions: This is an important section in any paper. Here usually the objective of the work is reiterated followed by the inferences/conclusions drawn from the present work. In many cases, scope for further work is also given here.

(h) References or Bibliography: Complete details of the reference cited in the paper are given in the order of their citation. Each journal/conference prescribes their format for this section and it should be adhered. Other references are furnished at the end, if they are important but not cited in the text. Today it is compulsory to cite the website addresses, if they are used in the work. Usually citations are made by numbers either enclosed with in the square brackets [] or as superscripts.

(i) Appendix (ces): Many times it may not be possible to furnish complete information in the main text as it may deviate from the main objective, however their presence in the text may help to understand the present work. All these are presented in the Appendix (ces). They may be derivation of some formula, wide spread data, component details or additional explanation on some point etc.

Finally it is the responsibility of the author(s) to acknowledge their institution, funding agencies etc, following the protocol. Many times funding agencies demand that their affiliation, sanction letter numbers, date of sanction to be indicated in acknowledgement.

After completing all the above steps it is very much essential to revise the complete paper in final form, to correct the language, continuity etc.. If possible obtain third person opinion. In some institutions there is a standard practice to conduct open seminar(s) before sending any paper for publication. This enables the author(s) to get value based feedback.

Significance of Recording the Observations

Information in any form will never go as waste. Valid data recorded will come to use if not now, in future. This can be visualized in the present day strategy of starting new power plants, guidelines to fishermen, military strategies, weather forecasting, share market fluctuations etc. Famous

Monte-Carlo technique, a well established scientific theory today was derived from the experience recorded by unknown gamblers, horse race addicts. Our numerology and astrology are also based on the available raw data recorded by many people earlier.

Few well accepted data processing/presentation techniques are furnished below to narrate the success story of recording data and/or observations.

1. Weather forecasting: Prediction of rain, cyclones, guidelines for fishermen etc., are made today using complex statistical data analyses, prediction techniques. Satellites are widely used to collect information about the type of soil, underground water resources, temperature variation in the atmosphere for the above analyses. This forecasting has helped agriculturists, fishermen to a great extent, to plan their routine activities.
2. Electrical load prediction: Establishment of new power plants, maintenance scheduling of existing power plants, operation scheduling of different types of power plants (unit commitment), economic load dispatch, selecting proper tie line and estimation of spinning reserve of each power plant, mainly depends upon short, medium and long time load forecasting. All these forecasting essentially process connected load details, operating load factors, maintenance requirements of individual power plants and failure data analyses of power system components. Success of these activities totally depends upon the available data.
3. Famine study: Based on the available statistical data of weather in our country, today scientists have come to a common consensus that famine

has a 13 years cycle. From the history it is clear that the severity of famine is changing from one famine to another based on the prevailing environmental conditions. The study of the available famine data and those days prevailing atmospheric conditions, have revealed the fact that, if rains are failed for successive three years, chances of loosing rains in further years is bound to happen. Based on this theory last year, South Indian State Governments took rain seeding activities to break the monotony of rain failure. Today we are witnessing the outcome i.e. fairly good rains have been reported from all over South India. Once again credit goes to those who recorded the data in earlier years!

4. Poll Prediction: Today every common man is able to predict the current political scenario effectively in their own way. This is reflected in exit poll results. Using exit poll results media persons, experts predict the current scenario near to the reality.

Considering the above facts, one can foresee the advantages of reporting scientific/technical observations. It means the transformation of raw thought or raw data into a presentable observation.

Conclusions

Importance of design of experiment to test the raw or vague idea or processing existing data to arrive at meaningful inferences is discussed in this paper. Conversion of these observations into a scientific technical paper is furnished along with some examples.

ACKNOWLEDGEMENT

Authors wish to express their thanks to Dr. N.H. Ayachit, for motivating the thought. Thanks are also due to the authorities of SDMCET, Dharwad, for encouraging to write this article.

DISCUSSIONS

Q: "Do not dilute earlier results" means what?

A: While using the earlier results, the author should acknowledge properly. Also those results are to be used with research integrity and partial results should not be used to infer something.

Q: How to make a paper at M. Tech. Level as the time available is very less?

A: This problem is possible for fresh works taken. It's better that faculty give part of an on-going work for project.

18

TECHNICAL REPORT: SOME ISSUES

Ashoka H.S.
Faculty, Chemical Dept.,
S.D.M. College of Engg. & Tech.,
Dharwad- 580 002

Dr. V.M. Bankapur
Sr. Librarian,
S.D.M. College of Engg & Tech.,
Dharwad- 580 002

ABSTRACT

Transmission of message, by means of effective language is to achieve the predetermined objective of communication. Transmission of commercial, industrial or scientific facts or news to the intended users within the boundaries of a particular technical field is job of technical report. The Technical Report (TR) is a common written form to communicate and their findings. Each TR should focus on topic that is developed logically along with some clearly identified perspective. Proper presentation of contents including illustrations delineates the structure, characteristics of technical writing.

Introduction

Since time immemorial human beings started communicating thoughts and feelings. Some of the earlier known modes of communication were gesture, symbols and geometric patterns. Communication is derived from Latin term "Communicare" or "Communico" both means to share. It enables them to acquire, exchange, store, retrieve and process information. It is transmission of a message by the use of effective language to achieve a predetermined objective. Technical report is a kind of written document that presents technical data as objectively as possible in a simple, direct, concise and precise manner. A technical report may be a letter, an article, a research paper and operational manual, a news bulletin, a brochure and a book review. Other written forms of technical communication important to researchers are: grant proposal, white paper, extended Abstract, journal article, research monograph, conference proceedings, cover letter, letter of recommendation, and job application letter. Important oral communication forms include: conference presentation, technical lecture, telephone conversation, and job interview. The importance of such communication disseminates the findings to others to learn and benefit from the findings.

A Technical Report should explain what you did, why you did it, what you discovered, and what is significant of your findings. The report should identify clearly what is novel about your work, and how it relates to prior knowledge. There should be a focused topic, and an attitude about this topic. The topic should be developed according to the attitude in a thorough, logical, and orderly fashion. Throughout, the author should be helpful to the reader.

The report should include the following components: descriptive title, author name and affiliation, date, informative Abstract, list of keywords, body, acknowledgments, and list of references. Additional separate appendices, where appropriate, may also be included. The standard four-part outline for the body of a technical report is motivation, methods, results, and discussion.

There is no minimum or maximum length requirement—the length should be appropriate for what you have to say. Many Technical Reports are about 10—20 pages long, but it is not uncommon for Technical Report to be significantly longer. Regardless of length, it is usually an effective strategy to explain in successive "layers." For example, lengthy Technical reports often begin with a relatively short overview section for readers who wish an executive summary.

The Thesis

Every Technical Report should have a *thesis*—a topic together with an attitude about the topic. The attitude helps focus the subject and provide a framework along which the topic subject can be explored. For example, the topic might be partitioning algorithms for the geometric Steiner tree problem, and the attitude might be that Steele's theory of Euclidean functional provides a powerful tool for analyzing the performance of such approximation algorithms. The introduction of each technical report should clearly identify its thesis and an organizational plan for developing the thesis.

The Components of Technical Report

A technical report should include each of the following items:

1. A logical, accurate, descriptive, and grammatically correct title:

   Titles should be as short as possible, while still satisfying the foregoing criteria. Avoid cute titles that violate these criteria. Two-part titles may be preferred because they provide short and long forms (e.g. "Statistical Techniques for Cryptanalysis: An Experimental Study using Real and Simulated English"). Avoid titles that exceed more words.
2. Author name and affiliation, and date. For example,

your affiliation might be 'Department of Computer Science and Engineering, University of Mumbai'. You might also like to include the city and state of your affiliation, your email address, and a URL of home page.

3. An informative Abstract of approximately 200 words: Make sure that your Abstract is informative—your Abstract should serve as a substitute for your paper. Briefly summarize your main findings. Concretely summarize; do not introduce. Immediately get to the point in the first sentence. Do not cite any references in the Abstract, and do not begin the Abstract with the weak, hackneyed, and boring phrase "This paper ...". The Abstract should be informative yet understandable to most researchers in your general field. The Abstract to fit on one title page, including the title, author name and affiliation, date, and list of keywords.
4. A list of appropriate keywords: These keywords should identify the field of your report and its major topics. Choose keywords to be helpful to researchers in locating your work in document-retrieval systems. What words and phrases should someone use to find your report? Be specific, and use only standard phrases. Browse some computer science journal (e.g. Journal of Algorithms) to get a feel for what is an appropriate keyword and what is not. *Computing Reviews* publishes an annual classification system including keywords which many journals follow.

   Many journals use three levels of keywords: general terms (e.g. cryptology), subject descriptors (e.g. differential cryptanalysis) recognizable to most researchers, and implicit terms—specific words or phrases that act as proper names (e.g. RSA Cryptosystem) which might not be recognizable to all readers.

5. Body of technical report: Write a clear, informative, and thoughtful description and critique of what you did. Where appropriate, include carefully drawn graphs and diagrams. Be sure to motivate, present, and interpret your findings.

   Focus on the scientific content of the project—your questions and answers. Identify and explain interesting and important phenomena. Emphasize what is new about the project. In addition, briefly comment on the engineering aspects of the work: what problems did you face, what decisions made, and what are the consequences of the decisions? Although it is crucial to explain your experimental procedures, be concise and do not bore your reader with lengthy descriptions of routine implementation concerns.

   Pay attention to important transitional sentences, especially the first and last sentences of the report. There are three standard ways to begin the introduction: startling statement, dramatic incident, and quotation. Try to end each report with a powerful sentence that concisely summarizes the significance of the entire project.

6. Acknowledgments: Acknowledge any help you received, including any use of computer equipment. Be specific.

7. Complete and accurate list of references cited in the technical report: There are three reasons for citing works: to give credit where credit is due, to be helpful to the reader to identify useful related

work, and to identify he context and background of your work. Adopt a bibliographic style used by some major refereed computer science journal (e.g. use the style for the \it Journal of the ACM\).

8. References by alphabetical order of author name: When citing references in the body of the report, always explain why the reference is being cited. For example, do not cite previous work without critically explaining how it relates to your work. In some cases the mention the author name in the textual citation, followed by the corresponding reference number (e.g. "In 1976, Diffie and Helman [14] proposed the concept of public-key cryptography.") is followed.

9. Appendices: These are for supplemental information and for information that is too detailed or voluminous to fit into body of the technical report. For example, a project involves any computer programming; you should include a nicely documented and formatted listing of all source code you write.

Organization of Technical Reports

A good technical report should have systematic organization. The body of the report along with the following points;

- motivation
- methods
- results
- discussion.

This will be helpful to separate logical organization from explicit numbered sectioning. For logical organization, the terms of hierarchies, part of the organizational task is to embed the logical organization into numbered sections. For example, the logical introduction might include one or more numbered sections, depending on what needs to be said. The report should be normally organized as

1. Introduction. A longer report might begin with a more elaborate logical introduction consisting of four numbered sections.
2. Overview.
3. Background.
4. Previous work. As the report evolves you may wish to modify the organization.
5. Describing the purpose of your project, restrict yourself to scientific and engineering reasons;
6. Conclusion, you should explain what it all means to you. If you discuss philosophy, do so in the discussion section.

Procedures in Experimental Findings

Explaining procedures to present results and to interpret results, summarize findings in meaningful ways, visualizing important data (e.g. in graphs) whenever possible. Experimentally measuring the running time of a computer program, test program on many randomly chosen inputs of a variety of sizes, including large inputs. Since the behavior of program might vary significantly among inputs of the same size, for each input size, try several inputs of that size and report the sample mean and standard deviation for that size; do not simply try one input per size. Explain procedures in sufficient detail so that other researchers can verify and replicate the findings.

Delivery Forms

A good report can have the following

1. Technical reports should have a standard 8.5 x 11 inch paper, with exactly one staple in the upper-left corner, without any cover. Source code or other appendices not to be attached to the main report. Avoid technical reports in binding, which simply add bulk.
2. Print any source code on 8.5 x 11 inch paper with carefully inserted page breaks. (i.e. separate the pages and arrange them like pages in a book) before handing in the listing.
3. In addition, make your report available on the WWW using your favorite hypertext language (e.g. html).

Evaluation of Technical Reports

Evaluatuation of Technical report on the basis of its scientific merit, effective presentation, and appropriateness for assignment. Evaluation thorough analysis, originality, and insightfulness. Scientific merit includes correctness, significance, novelty, non triviality, and completeness. Evaluate source code on the basis of its correctness, completeness, design, modularity, documentation, coding, user interface, and testing.

Common Mistakes to Avoid

Adhere carefully to the following guidelines:

1. In the introduction of your report, clearly identify a focused well-defined question. Answer this question in the rest of your report.
2. Analyze and interpret your data, and discuss the significance and limitations of your findings. Do not simply report your data.
3. Technical report is complete in the sense that it has each of the following components: descriptive

title, author name and affiliation, date, informative Abstract, list of keywords, body, acknowledgments, and references.

4. Abstract should specifically and concretely state your findings; do not vaguely describe what you set out to do. Your Abstract should summarize, not introduce. do not begin Abstract with the hackneyed phrase "This paper".

Documentation

Prepare a written report using a document preparation system. Such systems enable you to edit your document the numerous times required to create excellent prose. In addition, they will enable you to produce high-quality printed output. If you do not already know such a system, now is a good time to learn. The Latex system because it and its relative TEX produce high-quality results for mathematical typesetting, and Latex provides high-level document support (e.g. indexing and cross referencing). As for text editors, recommend Gnu Emacs because it is powerful, extensible, customizable, and self-documenting. For drawing graphs and doing statistical analysis of your data, recommend the program like xmgr, which runs on the SGI workstations.

Whenever working on a large project, you should save your notes and preliminary drafts. Many people find this material useful, and it will be helpful to you if you are ever challenged to show that the work is your own. In addition, you should keep a copy of the final report in case the original is lost.

Conclusion

The technical reports communicate the findings. A systematic organization of finding and presenting them to the intended users is the purposes of these media. It is transmission of a message by the use of effective language to achieve a predetermined objective. Proper organization with different components involved and evaluation are some of the aspects which help to write good technical reports.

REFERENCES

1. Miller, Casey, and Kate Swift, *The Handbook of Nonsexist Writing*, Harper and Row.
2. Krishna Mohan & Bannerji, Developing Communication Skills, Macmillan India Ltd 1990.
3. Sherman, Alan T., *"How to solve and write up homework problems"* (January 29, 1991).
4. Higham, Nicholas J., *Handbook of Writing for the Mathematical Sciences*, SIAM Press (1993).
5. Dornan, Edward A.; and Charles W. Dawe, *The Brief English Handbook*, Little, Brown and Company (1984).
6. *Letitia Baldrige's New Complete Guide to Executive Manners*, Rawson Associates (NY, 1993).
7. Strunk, William Jr.; and E. B. White, *The Elements of Style*, Macmillan (New York, 1972).

DISCUSSIONS

Q: What is the meaning of the term 'Report' in your presentation?

A: Common meaning whatever it has.

Q: Completely avoiding mathematical details in technical paper is sometimes impossible. Comment.

A: Include the details if inevitable. However, care should be taken towards avoiding complexities.

COMMENTS

International Patenting Authority prescribes "type of recording" to safeguard intellectual property rights.

19

WRITING TEXT BOOKS AND LABORATORY MANUALS

Dr. S.S. Bhavikatti
Professor & Head , Civil Dept.,
S.D.M. College of Engg. & Tech.,
Dharwad- 580002

ABSTRACT

The ability of a student to learn the subject to the required depth in prescribed time limit is to be assessed by test and examinations and this ability is to be quantified. This is done by awarding marks, certificates and degrees. Imparting sufficient knowledge in prescribed time limit is possible by making good books available to students. Experienced teachers should take up this job seriously and write good books and laboratory manuals. Author has presented some tips for writing them.

Introduction

The things taught in schools and colleges are not an education, but the means of education. The object of education is to prepare the young to educate themselves throughout their lives. But in this vast world, society needs certificates from impartial bodies to recognize to what level a person has achieved ability to learn. This part is done by examination boards and the universities. This is to be done in a rigid time schedule. Hence in the present system of awarding degrees, there is rigid syllabus, rigid time schedule and rigid examination system. Though examination system is often criticized, alternate system is yet to be evolved. To impart basic knowledge in any specified topic in specified time limit, good books are required for the students and it is the responsibility of the teachers to make such books available. In this paper author gives some tips for writing books and laboratory manuals.

When to Write

In his first 15 to 20 years of teaching career a teacher should concentrate on improving his teaching skills, acquiring more and more knowledge by involving himself in higher studies. research and consultancy. During this period he understands the difficulties of the students in studying the subject within stipulated time frame. Valuation of sessional tests and university examinations give good experience for the teacher to understand the students' difficulties. After age of about 45 years, the ability of teacher for self research reduces, but he turns out to be a good guide. At this age a teacher can consolidate his experience and write good books.

Preparation for Writing Books

Preparation for book writing starts with preparation of lecture notes. It includes revision of lecture notes, collection of syllabi of various universities and collection of question bank.

Preparation of Lecture Notes

It is always better to write detailed lecture notes since it helps in streamlining the presentation maintaining the continuity of thoughts, notations and method of presentation. For preparing lecture notes on any topic the teacher has to go through the syllabus and the previous question papers to decide the depth and scope of the topic. After reading 3 to 4 books, start thinking how to present own lecture. A student finds interest in the lecture, if he can find answers to various questions asked in the previous examinations.

Lecture notes should be written in good sheets using different colored pens. Identify the method of writing title of the topic, main articles, sub articles and the method of references to figures and published articles. It should be followed throughout the notes as if a book is being written. Lecture notes are to be written article by article after closing the various books referred. By any chance if some thing is directly taken from a book it should be noted. Various steps in deriving equations are to be numbered. Sketches should be drawn neatly. Always think of students and their level of understanding. Simple language should be used throughout.

In case of numerical problems, the problem should be stated completely as it is desired in the question papers. After writing one or two lines about approach to the problem, solve it thoroughly without skipping any step. Units should be indicated for the values obtained.

The problems selected should be arranged in order of increasing degree of difficulty. One or two lines may be written about how to tackle new degree of the difficulty. Lecture notes should contain little more examples than those which can be solved in available lecture time. Many problems may be discussed, clues given and students asked to solve themselves. However it is necessary to give final answers.

Revision of Lecture Notes

Many drawbacks of lecture notes will come to notice while teaching. These points should be noted in the class or immediately after the class. Additional notes may be appended. If the numbers of additional notes are too many, revised notes are to be prepared.

Writing the Book

The format of writing the book should be decided well in advance. Titles, sub titles, equation numbering and numbering of the figures are to be maintained throughout the same. Standard notations are to be used. The book writing scheme is to be worked out from whole to part. Decide the scope of the book, break it into suitable number of chapters and then take up writing it chapter by chapter. Each chapter should have a brief introduction, suitable number of sub titles and conclusions. Content of each chapter is to be decided after thoroughly going through the syllabi and the question papers of various universities. Lecture notes, if required with slight additions, can go into the contents of the book. At the end of chapter it is better to point what else can be referred for details of the subject, beyond the syllabus.

Writing Laboratory Manuals

It is necessary to have standard manuals for all practical subjects. In the absence of good reference manuals, students are likely to be guided by laboratory records of their seniors. This will result in falling standards year by year. Hence experienced teachers should take up writing laboratory manuals. If not for all classes, at least in the beginning of the engineering course, standard laboratory manuals should be made available so that students are exposed to proper method of writing their laboratory records.

About an Experiment

One should know the following about the experiments conducted

1. What is the aim?
2. What is the relevant theory?
3. What are the relevant standard codes?
4. What are the equipments and accessories required?

5. How to conduct the experiment?
6. What are the calculations to be made?
7. What are the graphs to be drawn?
8. What is the usual range of the values?
9. What are the limitations of the experiment / theory?
10. What alternate methods are there?
11. How to interpret the results?
12. Where to apply the results?

The Report

Report of an experiment should include answers for all the questions listed above. This takes the following form

1. Title and Date

The title of the experiment should be kept as brief as possible and should be written at the top. Date of experiment should be recorded without fail.

2. Object

If should be stated clearly and concisely.

3. Apparatus

The apparatus used should be described with neat diagrams, preferably on separate plain papers.

4. Theory

Definitions to new technical terms used must be given and the relationships which are to be verified must be stated.

5. Procedure

This is the description of how the test is carried out. The passive voice is to be used to write it.

6. Results

All the observations are to be tabulated and calculated results shown clearly. Specimen calculations also should be shown. Wherever possible the observations should be expressed in graphical form and the results derived from these graphs. The observed points are to be shown clearly.

7. Discussions and Conclusions

This is the most important part of the report. Theoretical and experimental results may differ. In such situations the reasons for the differences should be identified and conclusions drawn.

8. Theory Questions

At the end of report of each experiment theory questions should be given to make clear

1. Limitations of experiment / theory.
2. Alternate methods.
3. Interpreting the results.
4. Applications of the results.

Conclusions

It is desirable to write standard books and laboratory manuals so that students can grasp the maximum in the limited time available for studying a subject and face the examinations confidently. They should also get an idea that there is something more to be studied if the need be in their career.

DISCUSSIONS

Q: Why are you more satisfied as "Writer"?

A: Because I can serve larger community of students as writer. I receive positive response, recognition and appreciation by the unknown students also.

Q: Is it allowed to take matter from another book while writing books?

A: Taking, as it is, pages together, is not allowed. A portion (part of a page) can be taken. However it should be duly acknowledged.

THEME D

INSTITUTION MANAGEMENT AND CO-CURRICULAR ACTIVITIES

20

ORGANISATION CHARTS FOR A TECHNICAL INSTITUTE

Dr. Anand V. Shivapur
Asst. Professor, Dept. of Civil Engg.
S.D.M. College of Engg. & Tech.,
Dharwad- 580002
E mail **av_shivapur@rediffmail.com**

ABSTRACT

The achievement of the goals as mentioned in institute vision statement through the mission set is possible only by way of systematic organizational set up drawn by the institute. Only the best of the best-coordinated efforts will bring laurel to the institute and position it in the list of esteemed institutes in the region. In the present paper, author has made an effort to suggest suitable organizational patterns that help in achieving the end goal.

Key Words: Organizational Chart, Dean, Dutics, Responsibilities.

Introduction

The efficient working of any organization depends on how well the duties and responsibilities are legibly defined without any ambiguity for any administrative matters. Once an organizational setup and hierarchy is mentioned then duties and jobs to be carried out by each one will have to be stated. There should not be any scope for misinterpretation by any member of the executive in making decision. Hence it is not only necessary to draw the organizational setup, it is equally important to fix the job and responsibilities of every member concerned. However in the present paper, author has drawn organizational set up to be implemented up to certain level of administration viz. Heads of various department and heads of various activities.

Administrative Hierarchy at Institute Level

The efficient running of any organization as mentioned earlier depends on administrative hierarchy. While producing a suitable set up, a vision and mission of the institute has to be given prime importance. This should be such that there should not be any overlap of duties and responsibilities of individual heads of the particular departments. Keeping in view of the above aspects, the author has proposed a chart of organizational chart as shown in Fig.1.

Roles and Responsibilities of Various Heads

The following are few of the important responsibilities to be carried out by various heads of the departments in any organization/institute.

Secretary/Advisor

The Secretary/Advisor is a link between a management and the principal. He should be able to implement the service rules of working groups in the institute in addition to making efforts to solve any issues or disputes arising while taking any administrative decisions. He should put forth views of the faculty and others before the management/Government maintaining transparency at all level of implementation.

Principal

He is responsible for all matters of administration concerning staff and students of the institute, academic and all other matter in connection with smooth administration of the institution. He should plan for activities such as admission

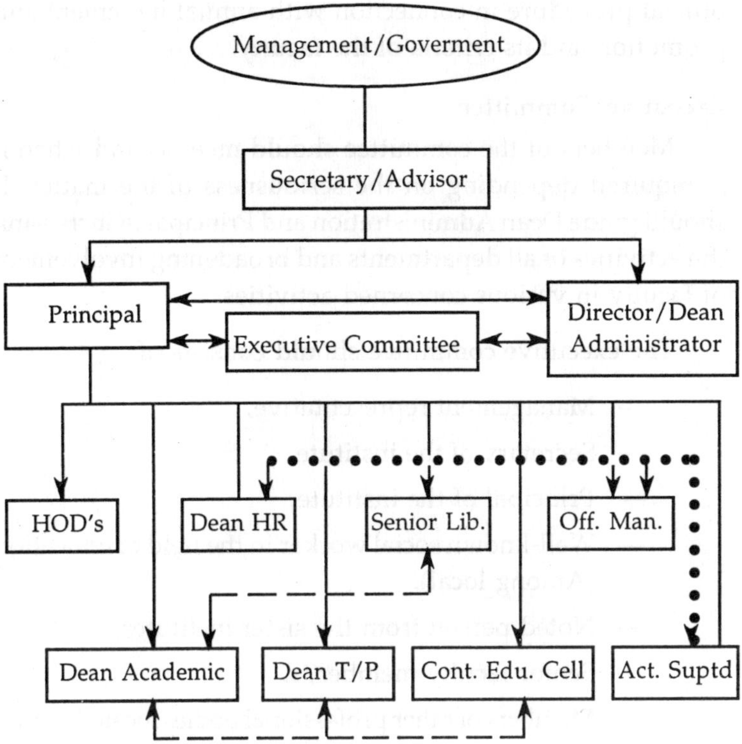

Fig. 1. Organizational Chart at Institutional Level

procedure, academic and cultural programs. He should have a thorough knowledge about how to elevate the standards of education to make the institution as an autonomous institute in addition he should pursue the matters connecting various funding agencies etc. He should inspire the staff and students to acquire higher education.

Director/Dean administration

Director / Dean Administration should formulate guide lines for the smooth conduct of all official and administrative procedures. He should do follow up action of some of the official procedure in connection with annual increment and promotion and its criteria of the faculty.

Executive Committee

Members of the committee should meet as and when it is required depending on the seriousness of the matter. It should guide Dean Administration and Principal in increasing the activities of all departments and broadening involvement of faculty in various concerned activities.

The executive committee should consists of

- — Management representative,
- — Secretary of the institute,
- — Principal of the institute,
- — Well-known social worker in the field of education (Among local),
- — Noted person from the sister institutes,
- — Senior faculty member/s.
- — Members of other professional bodies located within the jurisdiction of the institute.

Head of the Department

He should take into confidence all the members of the department. He is responsible for the smooth conduct of classes and other activities that are carried out at department level. He should inspire and take a follow up action so that individual staff member should be able to achieve their goal. He should be able to guide the in-charges of various committees that fall in his/her jurisdiction.

The organizational chart proposed at HOD level is as given below.

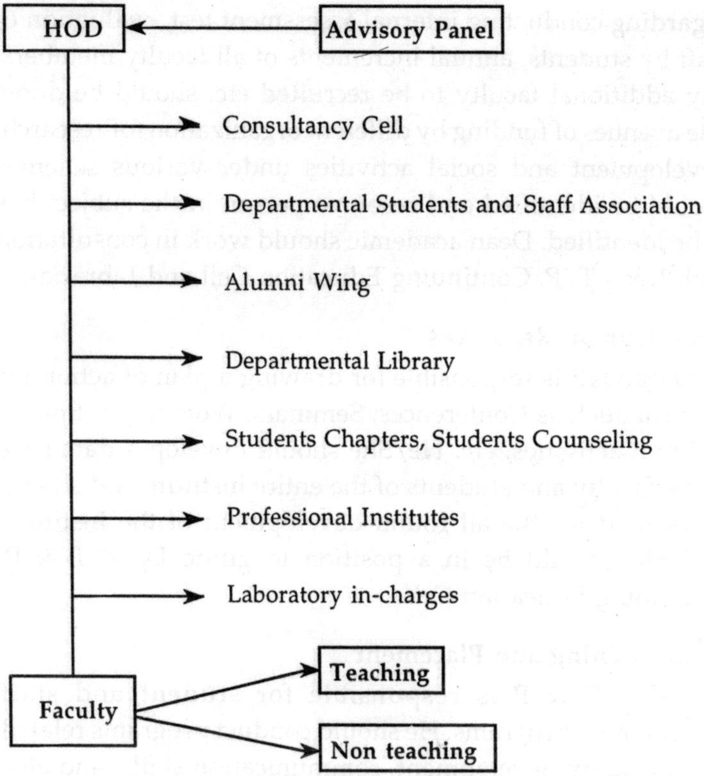

Fig. 2. Organizational Chart at HOD Level

Advisory Panel

Advisory panel should consist of few representatives from industries and neighboring well-recognized institutions. It should also involve few alumni who can spare time and should be able to guide institute to alleviate its standard.

Dean Academic

Dean academic is responsible for drawing annual plan of working of the institution along with various activities to be carried out under various disciplines. The follow up action regarding conducting internal assessment test, evaluation of staff by students, annual increments of all faculty members, any additional faculty to be recruited etc. should be done. The avenues of funding by different organization for research, development and social activities under various schemes should be identified and resource person in the subject has to be identified. Dean academic should work in consultation with Dean T/P, Continuing Education Cell and Librarian.

Dean Human Resources

Dean HR is responsible for drawing a plan of action for the year such as Conferences, Seminars, Workshops, Sports, Cultural activities, etc. He/She should develop a data base of the faculty and students of the entire institute and should strive hard for the all round development of the institute. He/ She should be in a position to guide Dean T & P, Continuing Education Cell.

Dean Training and Placement

Dean T & P is responsible for student and staff development programs. He should conduct programs related to personality development, communication skills, and also certain technical training programs calling experts from various organizations. The training should include all aspects of theoretical skills and a practical solution to the situation. He should have the knowledge of what is required in the relevant field.

He should get information regarding expectation of the industries to absorb our products. Based on the expectations of the industry he should device special courses to train the students.

He should be able to develop good communication with the industries in connection with the requirement of the industries, time and type of graduates that industry requires etc. He should work for the 100% placement for the students who graduate from the institute.

Continuing Education Cell

It should prepare annual plan for conducting various activities according to the need and importance of the subject. It should conduct training programs obtaining funds from various organizations.

In the present paper duties and responsibilities of few of the administrators have only been discussed. However jobs and responsibilities to be carried out by each one in the institute also contributes to the development and reflects on its standards.

Conclusion

The paper highlights the importance of organizational set up and duties and responsibilities of the member involved in an institute for the smooth conduct of all matters connected to administration, etc. The points mentioned in the paper, help only as a guide line. However an organization set up to be drawn is based on goal and objective of any institute.

DISCUSSIONS

Q: Most of the proposals are already being practiced in our college. What's the difference in your proposal?

A: I do not agree with your statement. Though there might be some rules, the organization chart does not exist and roles & responsibilities are not clearly defined. The jobs, responsibilities are to be clearly defined keeping it in mind that there should not be overlap of duties. In the present system no executive committee & continuing education cell exists. The coordination between various heads is also not defined.

Q: Your definition of "director" and "rotation system for headship" need to be clarified.

A: The definition of 'director' goes with the vision and mission of institute. It depends on organization setup drawn for effective implementation towards reaching institute vision. The question of rotation system for headship does not come in organization setup. However, rotation system can come only when there are many people with required qualification and skill to take over various positions.

21

STRATEGIC MANAGEMENT OF INSTITUTIONS OF HIGHER EDUCATION

Prof. K. Balakrishnan
SDM Institute for Management Development, Mysore 570005
Ph: +91-821-2429722/161 Ext 23 Fax: +91-821-2425557
e-mail: sdmimd@vsnl.com / kondath_b@hotmail.com

ABSTRACT

Higher education in India has for long been in a state of considerable crisis. Many studies have been conducted over the decades, but there is a material change since the seventies and eighties in that a number of private players have entered the scene. Options for improving the relevance and quality of higher education have since increased, with innovative models of management with a demonstrated record of success. However diffusion of good management practices has been perfunctory, at best. This is especially true when we consider institutions of higher technical education and in the humanities areas. There have been many hurdles placed by the educational bureaucracy, but there are also obstacles placed by unfeeling and unthinking managements. While the lack of appropriate ambition or a value framework is a different issue, in the context of general liberalization there is scope for professionalisation of management processes in educational institutions. This paper considers approaches and techniques apposite to the management of any institution engaged in imparting higher education.

Considerable attention is being paid now to the admission process and costs of engineering medical and management education, thanks mainly to certain Supreme Court decisions. However the entire gamut of the managerial process in institutions of higher education (HE) needs attention. This paper tries to work out an approach to management of such institutions including certain techniques on the assumption that managements are serious in maintaining quality and relevance.

1. Scope and Context

A commonly accepted definition of 'technique' is it is "part of an artistic skill that is reducible to a formula." In the management world a few such techniques are PERT/CPM, LP, DCF, 360 Feedback, Segmentation etc. At this stage considering only techniques is too reductionist in scope and therefore, this paper will develop an "Approach to the Strategic Management of Institutions of Higher Education (Is/ HE)." We will therefore not be considering issues concerning the management of primary and secondary education institutions.

1.1. Let us first look at the context of HE in India. HE programmes and institutions can be classified into

- Undergraduate, Post Graduate, Doctoral & Research Programmes
- UGC system of affiliating & unitary universities
- MCI, Dental Council, AICTE & Bar Council Universities
- Deemed Universities
- IIMs, IITs, IISc, etc.,
- Independent Institutions; to which can be added the new phenomenon of
- Foreign Universities

1.2. Before we consider possible approaches to management of HE institutions, we need to step back and consider the problems & issues[21] peculiar to H. E. in India[3,14]. The specificities are well known and needs no enumeration, but it must be noted that the locus of the most recalcitrant ones lie within the UGC system, & have been recognized as such for at least the last 40 years. Several attempts at reform have been made – the Dr. S. Radhakrishnan & D. S. Kothari Commissions, the New Educational Policy[15] of the early nineties et al, but the net result is that of comprehensive failure in reform. Without elaborating too much, the manifestation of this problem of failed reform is in poor quality of input, poor quality of process & poor quality of output.[4]

1.3. This all pervasive lack of quality affects all institutions of HE in India in various ways, and must be taken into account when we consider a managerial approach. There are four fundamental truths that are apposite and we will consider each one briefly. We must however bear in mind that these fundamental truths should be seen not in isolation, but in interplay.

1.4. The *first fundamental truth* is that quality in any system is dependant on the demand characteristic of the downstream link in the value / process chain. For HE, the downstream link is of two types:

- Industry
- Research / Teaching Institutions

Those H.E. institutions that have the greatest co-ordination with the downstream link and are most responsive to downstream requirements are therefore the 'better' ones. This explains partially the relative success of the IITs, IIMs, IISc or the

BARC Training School.

1.5. The *second fundamental truth* is that in the Indian ethos, the predominant ideology of education is transmission, with little role for the interpretation & autonomous ideologies. A little reflection will tell us why this is so. Memorization has had a very honorable place in Indian educational learning over the ages. Witness for a contemporary illustration, B.R Chopra's TV serial Mahabharata, where in a memorable scene in the court of King Dhritirashtra, one of the courtiers accepts the challenge of reciting the names of all the 100 Kauravas in correct order of primogeniture. This is illustrative of all preliterate societies which believe that erudition consists in the ability to recall & display knowledge. In modern times, the direct consequence of this is the university examination system which places a high premium on rote & recall.[2,7,20]

1.6. The *third fundamental truth* recognizes the need to distinguish between manifest & latent functions[5] of any social institution. While manifest functions are articulated, measured & analyzed, the latent function of HE in India is to provide the state a 'cooling off' period – this explains why, while the state does not achieve targets in education for various objectives, the targets for establishment of UG Colleges in semi-urban & rural areas are systematically over- achieved.[5, 17]

1.7. The *fourth fundamental truth* arises from an extension of one of my current research interests – which is the study of network systems theory in management[1, 16]. The HE Scenario in India with all its constituent parts can be visualized as a network in its own right. We know from the study of networks that their health is dependant on successful boundary maintenance. Boundary maintenance prevents & fights the entry of foreign bodies into the network, while the UGC system exhibits the entry of politicians, bureaucrats, policemen & plain criminals, all with various vested interests. This view of H.E as a network system implies that we can model it with nodes, hubs & links. Further, the system exhibits the existence of a power law, a non-normal distribution. Other properties that characterize such a network are its scale-free nature, with directed paths, forced preferential attachments, distance dependence, and the characteristic fitness distribution that determine its topology. I will not go into details of the theoretical derivation of these concepts to the HE network but it is enough to keep them in mind when we consider a managerial approach for Is/HE.

1.8. In this approach, every institution of HE is considered a node / hub, connected by a link to another node / hub which could be the university, UGC or AICTE. Incompetence in boundary maintenance on the part of the hubs also affects the nodes. The managerial task / objective for the Is HE are therefore to preserve its own integrity in an environment of network collapse.

2. A Framework

2.1. Keeping these fundamental truths in mind, the basic assumption that we make here is that the owners / founders of the / HE seek to establish, maintain & promote 'quality' – without this basis, there is no analysis. We further assume that it is possible for an HE to seek an ROI without necessarily getting 'commercialised'.[8,12]

2.2. The first step is to recognize the need for & institute a formal strategic management process. The owner/ founders need to articulate a well considered vision & mission for the institution. This then needs to be further elaborated into long-term objectives (LTOs). While the mission & LTOs for elite institutions such as the IIMs, IITs, IISc etc., would differ from those enunciated for undergraduate colleges, vision statements for both categories should recognize the need for excellence & professionalism.

2.3. Who should be involved in this process of developing & articulating the mission, vision & LTOs? Apart from the owner / founders, there should be active participation from top management (the Director / Principal & the Chief of Administration) the Faculty & select Alumni. All too often, a recurring complaint in Is/HE is the non-responsiveness of the administration to the requirements of the teaching staff. In every such situation there are usually deep-seated process-related & structural reasons for this phenomenon. Lack of participation of the bureaucracy in higher strategy / policy formulation is one of them.

2.4. The next step is for the top management & faculty to jointly evolve a philosophy of education that must be peculiar to the institution & its mission. We had earlier referred to the 3 ideologies of transmission, interpretation & autonomy. The philosophy of education of the HE should explicitly recognize that every part of this ideology spectrum has its own role to play. Given below is a model of application.

Ideology / Institution	Transmission	Interpretation	Autonomy
UG	**High**	**Medium**	**Low**
PG	**Medium**	**High**	**Medium**
Research	**Low**	**High**	**High**

Fig. 1. Model of Education – Ideology Application to Institutions of Higher Education

2.5. This philosophy then becomes the basis for 4 core pedagogical activities of curriculum design, content development, content delivery and evaluation.

2.6. The application of this philosophy is also closely linked to the concept of the three parallel systems of processing information whose relative importance also varies with one's position on the ideology spectrum[13]. The first of these is the ***'enactive'*** representation of knowledge, which is learning by doing. At one end this is the kindergarten child playing with blocks on interlocking puzzles, and at the other the management graduate analyzing a case or working on a summer project ; the chemistry major watching a reaction in the lab, or the biology student dissecting a frog. The second system is ***'ikonic'*** representation where we use a pictorial representation to describe an idea or a concept. Management models are described thus, so are plans of buildings under construction. The third way is ***'symbolic'*** representation were we define a square as "a set of sets such that the number of elements in each set is equal to the number of sets" or where we define a straight line in Euclidian space as the shortest distance between two points or when we simply say, $E = mc^2$.

2.7. The point is, the core pedagogical activity of content delivery has to employ the appropriate mix of these 3 systems.[15,18,19]

2.8. We next turn to the question of organization design. A good generalized organization model is visualized as a double triangle – the outer one composed of structure, people & strategy bound together by the inner triangle of process. Such a scheme incorporates the inherent strength of the triangle and also the fact that weakening any links weakens the whole.

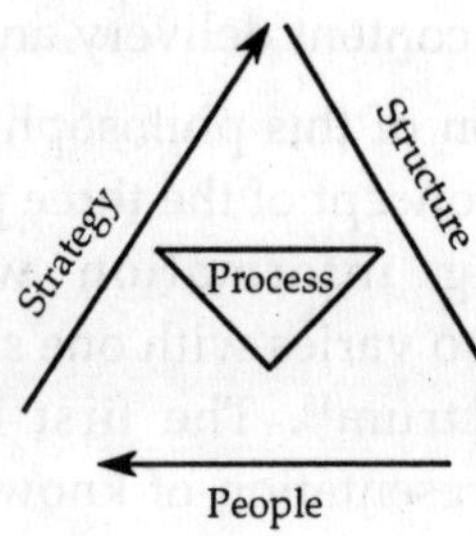

Fig. 2. Organization Model for HE

3. The Elaboration

3.1. We will now consider each of these four elements. The aim of strategy development for the IHE is to obtain answers to 4 sets of related questions

- 'In what areas <u>are</u> we in? *should / want* to be in? and *do not* want to be in ?'
- 'Where do the inputs to the system come in from? What are its characteristics?'
- 'Where do our outputs go? What is the downstream link in the (value) chain ?
- 'What does the downstream link in the process chain want ?'

3.2. The aim of the organizational structure is to provide the necessary balance between the differentiation & integration needs of the HE & to play a positive role in the development of a functional institutional culture. Structure will address the relative positions of the owner / founders, the top management, the faculty & the administrative staff. In designing this structure, the fundamental principle to be kept in mind is the primary of Pedagogy over Administration.

3.3. We can consider a number of suggestions in this area. The head of the institution, the Director or Principal, should by and large be internally selected. Exceptional situations could be when the HE is just being set up, or there is an acute paucity of faculty. Internal selection, should however be the norm & obviously be restricted from among the faculty. Further, there should be a clear non-extendable 5 year term for the Head, with an Associate / Deputy Head being chosen half way through the tenure of the Head. One the system is well established, we expect to see the Associate / Deputy take over leadership at the end of 2 ½ years. There is thus continuity along with change with the new Head being completely aware of issues concerning the management of the HE. The 'retired' Head meanwhile, continues as an ordinary faculty member.

3.4. A similar arrangement holds good for Faculty / Department / Area Chairman. The principle of selection should be rotation within the concerned discipline, with a non-extendable 3 year term and eligibility for every faculty member with a minimum of 3 years service in the concerned department.

Here again, once the term is over, the HOD reverts to the position of the ordinary faculty member. Notice however, that this arrangement breaks the inflexible link between Headship & seniority. A Reader or Associate Professor is just as likely to become HOD for a term as a long serving full Professor.

3.5. The aim of structural reform is to displace the locus of faculty job satisfaction and motivation from hierarchical progression to opportunity for personal professional development – research, writing papers, attending conferences and conducting seminars.

3.6. This type of structure is just as feasible for a UG College, as it is for elite institutions, provided there is a will. The advantage of this arrangement is that it promotes the development of cross-functional teams and represents a paradigm shift from the view of management as a phenomenon punctuated by a change of Director, to management as driven by an engineered process.

3.7. Let us now look at issues concerning management of human resources of the HE. There are five basic tasks in this area

- Communicating the Mission & Vision to all levels
- Mapping required competencies to input profile & output specifications
- Building necessary skills & attitudes
- Recognition of effort and achievement
- Talent Acquisition, Reward & Denial

3.8. What needs to be kept in mind is that these tasks are common across all grades & departments –

faculty as well as administrative staff. Because faculty are supposedly professionals first who plan and execute their own professional development, Is/HE have typically not addressed internal HR issues in any systematic manner, even in management institutions where HR itself is a field of study. This is akin to an engineering college constructing its campus not by consulting its civil engineers, but by being put together by the local sand & cement supplier.

3.9. Various approaches & techniques are available for management of various aspects of the HR function. However the one integrated system, which with appropriate modification, can be implemented in Is/HE is the People Capability Maturity Model (P-CMM). Originally developed for the software industry, (which apart from educational / research institutions is the other knowledge industry) the model is now being adopted even by smoke stack organizations.. The model is depicted in Fig (2).

3.10. To consider now the inner interlocking triangle of our model – processes. Six basic processes constitute the heart of purposive management of any IHE

- Continuous up gradation of knowledge
- Continuous measurement of performance
- Continuous innovation in pedagogy
- Continuous revision of course content
- Continuously responsive administration
- Continuous feedback systems

3.11. Continuous up gradation of knowledge is the key here. While PG and Research Institutions undertake this to a large extent, it is conspicuous by its absence in the UG sector. There are many reasons for this.

Lack of adequate financial resources and the nature, quality and objectives of inputs are the most salient ones. For teaching purposes however, subscribing to just one good international journal per discipline will start a chain reaction provided it is integrated into the learning process irrespective of UGC/ University curricula.

3.12. The common thread running through these six processes is *change.* We need a model to evaluate

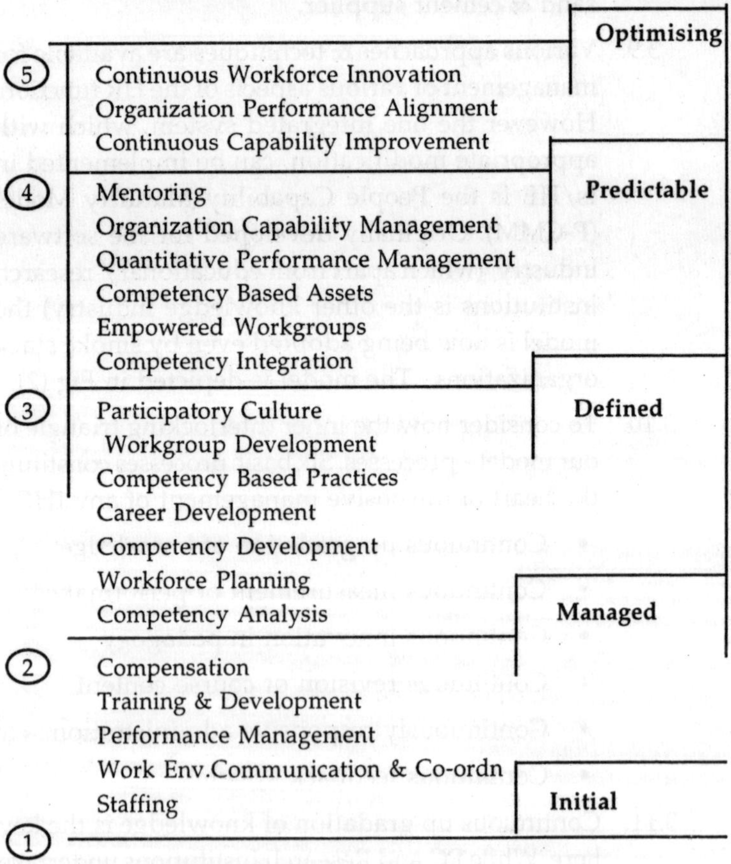

Fig. 2. Process Areas & Levels of the P-CMM Model

change, especially where change is a current development not susceptible to classical experimental design. One model looks at four types of evaluation: context, input, process & product. This is actually a systems approach, differing only in its rather flexible application to a discrete problem. The CIPP model can be applied to a new curriculum, to evaluating teaching methods or assessing community / industry involvement The CIPP Model is shown in Fig 3 below:[10]

3.13. For successful process management, it is necessary to identify the process owners and estimate the resources required and the outputs of the process. This will logically lead to the concept of the internal customer, where every employee and every department in the internal value chain is seen as the customer to the down stream link and a supplier to the upstream. Such a view of the process leads to a bottom-up approach to budget preparation. Management control is then exercised through culture, budgets and empowerment rather than through rules and bureaucracy.

3.14. Process maturity as described above leads to another challenge for top management. It is that while the internal customer concept and bottom-up budgeting are excellent tools to achieve participation, coordination and empowerment, it still does not guarantee the alignment of all departmental / individual goals to super ordinate ones. We know by experience, both in the corporate world and the world of social institutions that institutional failure is more often the result of ineffective strategy implementation rather than inefficient strategy formulation. The tool to resolve this is the Balanced Score Card.

	Context Evaluation	Input Evaluation	Process Evaluation	Product Evaluation
Objective	To Define the *operating context*, to identify and assess *needs* in the context, and to identify and delineate *problems* underlying the needs.	To identify and assess *system capabilities*, available input *strategies*, and *designs* for implementing the strategies.	To identify or predict, in process, *defects* in the procedural design or its implementation, and to maintain a record of *procedural events* and *activities*.	To relate *outcome information* to objectives and to context, input, and process information.
Method	By describing individually and in relevant perspectives the major subsystems of the context; by comparing actual and intended inputs and outputs of the subsystems; and by analyzing possible causes of discrepancies between actualities and intentions.	By describing and analyzing available human and material resources, solution strategies, and procedural designs for relevance, feasibility and economy in the course of action to be taken.	By monitoring the activity's potential procedural barriers and remaining alert to unanticipated ones.	By defining operationally, and measuring, criteria associated with the objectives, by comparing these measurements with predetermined standards or comparative and for interpreting bases, the out comes in terms of recorded context, information.
Relation to Decision Making in the Process	For deciding upon the *setting* to be served, the *goals* associated with meeting needs, and the *objectives* associated with solving problems, i.e., for planning needed changes.	For selecting sources of *support*, solution *strategies*, and procedural *designs*, i.e., for programming change activities.	For implementing and refining the program design and *procedure*, i.e., for effecting process control.	For deciding to *continue*, *terminate*, modify, or *refocus* a change activity, and for linking the activity to other major phases of the change process, i.e., for evolving change activities.

Fig 3. The CIPP Evaluation Model

3.15. The Balanced Score Card looks at the implementation of strategy from four perspectives

– the financial perspective, the customer perspective, the internal business process perspective and the learning and growth perspective. There is considerable awareness of this technique and so we will not go into further detail. Suffice it to say that a properly constructed Score Card is balanced between lagging indicators (such as pass rates) and appropriate leading indicators. All of them are linked in a cause and effect relationship back to the LTOs and mission of the organization. The BSC can therefore be the integrating technique in an HE.[11]

4 Production & Dissemination

4.1 Indian educational institutions, with some notable exceptions, have been content with mere dissemination of knowledge with little emphasis on production. Production of knowledge can be viewed as either creation of new knowledge or a new presentation or reorganization of the existing. We need to realize, however that at higher education levels, a certain modicum of participation in knowledge production has significant rub-offs in the quality of teaching itself. Opportunities will vary according to type and location of the institution, but it is possible for every faculty member to take some part in some type of production activity every year. Faculty evaluation should address this aspect but the best results will be achieved if knowledge production activities are undertaken as a result of an inner drive rather than an 'increment' drive. When institutionalized, however, peer pressure will usually work as an acceptable motivator.

5 End Game

5.1. Some final comments before conclusion. At the outset it had mentioned that while missions and LTOs would vary from one institution to another, the vision of each one must have something to do with excellence. What could be the main hurdles to building excellence? We venture to say that the biggest problem is the lack of vision at the owner / top management level. The greatest shortage in India is not in resources, opportunities or skills but of the passion for excellence. Without this nothing worthwhile is achievable.[22]

5.2. Today Indian society is in transition from a period of institution building to institution breaking. The Nehrus, Bhabhas and Sarabhais have given way to the extremist egocentric Babu and Neta. From Bhabha to Babu we are witnessing a continuously downward sloping curve. The clues to this phenomenon are to be found in the Indian ethos – where there is simply no room for succession planning in an orderly passion. From the Mauryan Empire, Ashoka, the Guptas, the Kushans, the Mughals to the post independence and pre dynastic Congress Party and the various regional parties, we see the institutions flourish alongside a charismatic leader, and a decline thereafter. Our structural framework for the HE consciously tries to avoid this pitfall.

5.3. The context of HE today is by and large the UGC framework with its overwhelming concern for uniformity and equivalence and a fascination for trivia. (The AICTE had a path breaking debate on whether the management programme should be designated as PGDMS, PGDBA or PGDBM). It is a network that not only exhibits dissolution of boundary maintenance but also proneness to cascading failures. On a day to day basis we in India experience cascading failures in another type of network – the State or Regional Electricity Grids. Where pockets of power supply continue to exist, they do so because of islanding – the concerned generating station simply cuts itself off from the grid. In HE cascading failures manifest itself in increasing irrelevance of its outputs to users. This is the inevitable conclusion when subornation of objectives takes place from the manifest to the latent.

5.4 The conclusion therefore is that for a quality conscious IHE, islanding is the only way out. We see it already happening and where it does we can recognize the excellence that exists. Computer education institutions such as NIIT & Aptech, AMIE, ICAI, ICWAI, ACS and ICFAI exemplify the virtues of islanding. On the other hand the IIMs and IITs are doomed to degradation in as much as political entrepreneurs make their entry into them[8]. Within governmental bodies we see the institutions that are saved by relatively better boundary maintenance – the Departments of Atomic Energy & Space.

5.5 For IsHE the only way out is to delink from degrees; establish, maintain and demonstrate quality and obtain market approval.

BIBLIOGRAPHY

1. Balakrishnan, K "Network Systems Theory, Quantum Mechanics, Globalization & Decentralization" Pragyaan, Vol 1, No 1, Jun 2003

Bloom, Benjamin S "Evaluation in Higher Education: A Report of the Seminars on Examination Reform Organized by the UGC under the Leadership of Dr. Benjamin S Bloom."

2. Cerych, Ladislav & Sabatier Paul, "Great Expectation & Mixed Performance : The Implementation of Higher Education Reforms in Europe (Stoke-on-Trent England, Trentham Books, 1986)
3. Chauhan C.P.S " Higher Education in India : Achievements, Failures & Strategies" (New Delhi, Ashish, 1990)
4. Clark, Burton R "The 'Cooling Out' Function in Higher Education" (American Journal of Sociology 65, May 1960)
5. Deva, Indra "Latent Functions of Higher Education in India" (Journal of Higher Education, 7, 1982)
6. Gilbert, Irene "The Indian Academic Profession : The Origins of a Tradition of Subordination" (Minerva 10, July 1972)
7. Glaser, Robert "The Education of Individuals" (Learning Research & Dev Center, U of Pittsburgh)
8. Indiresan P.V. & Nigam N C "The Institutes of Technology: Excellence in Peril"
9. Joyce, Bruce "Alternative Models in Education" (Waltham, Mass : Blaisdell Pub Co, 1968)
10. Kaplan, Robert S & Norton, David P "The Balanced Scorecard: Translating Strategy Into Action " (Boston: HBS Press 1996)
11. Mead, Margaret "Thinking Ahead" Why is Education Absolute?" (HBR, XXXVI, Nov – Dec 58)
12. Merton R.K. "Social Theory & Social Structure" (New York : Free Press 1968)
13. Nagai, Michio "Higher Education in Japan : Its Take-Off & Crash" (University of Tokyo Press 1971)
14. National Policy of Education 1986 – Program of Action" (MHRD, GoI, Nov 86)
15. Newman M.E.J., Strogatz S.H. & Watts D.J. "Random Graphs with Arbitrary Degree Distribution and Their Applications" (Physical Review, E64, 2001)
16. Pulparambil, John, "Stages of Institutional Decay : Some Aspects of Management Crisis in Educational Institutions" (Loyola Journal of Social Sciences V Jan 1991)
17. Rao T.V. "Planning & Management For Excellence in Education" (Working Paper No.865, IIMA, May 90)
18. Raza, Moonis "Higher Education in India – Retrospect & Prospect "(New Delhi, AIU, 1991).

19. Singh, Amrik "Examinations : The Strategy of Change" in "The Higher Learning in India" eds: Singh, Amrik & Altbach, Philip (New Delhi, Vikas 1974)
20. Swamy, Dalip S. & Raina, Badri N "Subversion of Universities" Seminar No.296 (Apr 84)
21. Udgaonkar B.M. "Future of the University System" (Journal of Education & Social Change in 1987)

DISCUSSIONS

Q: Whether performance index is context sensitive or not?

A: It is context sensitive. It is linked to strategy of institution.

Q: How to convey vision and mission in an environment of individuals with different tastes?

A: Conduct seminars, discussions, faculty meetings etc (effective points in vision and mission are usually two or three). In short increase communication.

Q: Won't there by any problems in having rotation of posts?

A: Care should be taken to avoid interference. Positive attitude is very much essential. There won't be any problems as proved by many individuals and institutions.

Q: Other than IIMS, IITS etc, the next link in the chain of studies and its utility not strong. How to meet this?

A: Individual College should grow on its own. Don't force common template. Students and staff can undergo training in the field of their interest.

Q: What is the difference between IAS and IIM products?

A: IAS students are trained for administration, whereas IIM students are trained for management. Their attitudes differ. However, there are exceptions.

22

GUIDANCE AND COUNSELING

C. M. Koti
Professor, Dept. of Mech. Engg.,
S.D.M. College of Engg. & Tech.,
Dharwad – 580 002

ABSTRACT

Teachers have to tackle many types of problems faced by students. Students will have problems at various stages such as before entry, at entry, during the program and after the exit. Assisting a student to solve his problems and help him to grow is all about guiding and counseling.

Guidance and Counseling

- Guidance is the assistance given by one individual to another individual or group to understand and solve problem and to assist him/ them to grow,
- Counseling is the assistance given by one individual to another in helping him to understand and solve his problem.

Outcomes of Guidance and Counseling

- To Teachers

  IMMEDIATE: New knowledge and skills related to the problem to be solved.

  INTERMEDIATE: Increased confidence and capabilities in solving complex problems.

LONG TERM: Increased capabilities for taking steps to prevent recurrence of Problems.

- TO STUDENTS

  Better adaptability and adjustment to new situations and environment, improved mental health, greater understanding and responsiveness.

- TO INSTITUTIONS:

  Improved cordial relation between teacher and taught, trouble free campus life, better utilization of institutional resources, healthy campus life, congruence in working styles, increased efficiency and effectiveness.

- TO SOCIETY

  Well adjusted and mentally sound Pass outs / Technicians / Engineers

Students' Problems

- Adjustment in new environment
- Classroom interaction
- Family interference
- Political interference
- Hostel adjustment
- Emotional problems
- Identity crisis (problem of belongingness)
- Addiction to smoking, tobacco etc.
- Future employment problems
- Changing value

Guidance and Counseling Principles

- G & C is unique to an individual
- It is considered with the total individual

- It is always goal oriented and goal directed
- Guidance is a professional activity
- It should be based on a through knowledge of characteristics of the developmental stages and environmental influences for an individual
- G & C is meant for all who need help
- C & C is a continuous process
- It should be based on reliable data obtained by using appropriate tools

Guidance and Counseling Objectives

- Assist students in overcoming their emotional, social and personal problems.
- Help students to realize maximum benefit from their stay in the educational institution.
- Create a harmonious atmosphere to facilitate teaching / learning.
- Buildup healthy inter and intra personal relation between peers, students and teachers.
- Make campus life peaceful and congenial.
- Enable teachers to identity different categories of problems of students and solve them satisfactorily.
- Organize student services to cater to the co-curricular and other requirements of students.
- Create an environment of mutual trust and understanding in students and teachers.

Suggested Educational Guidance Activities

- Organizing induction programs
- Maintaining an "Academic Master Register"
- Providing assistance to special learners

- To assist creative learners
- To conduct special classes, quiz etc.,

Suggested Career Guidance Activities

- Career talk
- Career conference
- Ability exploration session
- Training for interviews
- Career corner
- Industrial visits
- Consultant meeting
- Web based information

Suggested Personal – Social Guidance Activities

- Developing self confidence through assertiveness training
- Eradicating personal inadequacy through personality development programs
- Organizing human relations skills training programs
- Organizing counseling programs
- Organizing group guidance programs
- Use of T. M.
- Use of stress reduction models

Guidelines for Guidance and Counseling Center

- To formulate objectives of the centre,
- To identify activities to be organized,
- To procure / arrange resources,
- To identify personnel and allocate responsibilities,
- To draw the schedule of activities and decide target groups,

- To organize activities,
- To evaluate activities.

REFERENCE

Resource Material "Three days workshop on student Guidance and Counseling" conducted by VTU, Belgaum 2.08.04 to 4.08.04.

DISCUSSIONS

Q: How to tackle issues like change of branch wherein parents also have a major say?

A: Along with students, parents also need counseling and guidance.

Q: How mentorship differs from guidance?

A: Mentorship is an important part of guidance and counseling where Academic Master Register is developed and a faculty member comes to know the problems of a student. If possible, he himself can assist in solving the student problems; otherwise he can refer it to a competent person.

Q: Can every teacher perform "Counseling" and "Guidance"?

A: Yes! to some extent. At the beginning of his career it may be little difficult. But over the years one can acquire the skills required for guidance and counseling.

23

NSS AS A CO-CURRICULAR ACTIVITY

Sunilkumar S. Honnungar
Faculty, Mech. Dept. and NSS Program Officer
S.D.M. College of Engg. & Tech.,
Dharwad- 580002
Email : sunilhonnungar@yahoo.com.

ABSTRACT

In present educational system we see lot of loopholes in student community in understanding their responsibilities and involving themselves in academic activities. The overall personality development has not been given much importance in our curriculum due to changing technological pace. Even Indian youth have not seen a dynamic personality to give them guidance in right direction after swami Vivekananda nor got a proper platform to build their overall personality along with their academic activities. NSS is one such platform where the youth especially students community can shape themselves in to good future citizens as well become efficient in their profession. This paper narrates relevance and implementation of NSS in technical degree colleges.

Introduction to NSS

The National Service Scheme (NSS) was started in 1969, 24th September; Mahatma Gandhi Centenary year by Shri VKRV Rao an educationist and education minister in Karnataka state government. (Before this Dr. N. S. Hardikar of Karnataka state had already started Hindustan Seva Dala in the year 1923 keeping in mind for motivating youth for independence moment and almost during same time Dr. Hedgevar also started Rastriya Seva Sangh in Maharastra.) The focal objective of the scheme is the overall development of personality of students by providing them with opportunities to participate in the community development service programmes and enable them to acquire experience by exposure to the life outside educational institutions. The scheme has brought NSS volunteer in direct contact with the community problems, need and development processes. This enables them to plan and organize need-based programmes resulting in creation of tangible intangible assets. This scheme, started with student coverage of 40,000 in 1969, has expanded many folds and covers over 1.6 million students in the year 1998. The student volunteers through NSS have successfully participated in National Priority Programmes Like Total Literacy Campaigns, Health and Sanitation, Environment Awareness and Enrichment Programmes, Gender Equity, Self-Employment Income Generation Programmes, etc. Where NSS is integrated with the curriculum/academic programmes, it has helped to make education more relevant to community development, national goals, social and economic processes.

The Relevance of NSS in Technical Colleges

In technical degree colleges with semester system it is very much difficult to accommodate and bring importance to NSS due to compact and tight scheduled academic activities. This was the main reason why NSS was unpopular even in agriculture science professional course until it was resolved to have compulsory NSS activity with credits. (Agri-university of Dharwad has successfully implemented NSS in their curriculum as one compulsory subject with exam and other credits.) Of course for agricultural science it is very much relevant as their profession and NSS objectives go hand in hand. For us like technical colleges, we have to redefine the objectives of NSS and try to keep some credits to the volunteers if not to make compulsion.

Degree certificate gives assessment of intellectuality, but we don't have any assessment procedure to certify whether a person is developed fully in his personality or not. In present Liberalization, Privatization, Globalization scenario one should have Innovative skill, Analytical skill, Communication skill, Problem-solving skill, and Observation skill. Only NSS can provide platform for all these skills. In addition to all these skills NSS gives leadership qualities, group being, imagination, scarifies, culture, humanity, marketing skills which are most essential for a technical student. So it is very much relevant in present context to adopt NSS in technical colleges along with curricular activities.

Activities Management

We can manage NSS by conducting following activities:

- **Trekking**: This will help for exposure to the nature where students can learn more about eco balance, conservation of natural resources etc. Even self confidence and will power can be boosted through trekking. Now-a-days, will power and self-confidence are hardly understood by our young generation. We can see the school children asking for lifts while on their way to school. This shows their lack of attitude towards hard work and lack of sense of time management.
- **Blood Donation and AIDS awareness:** Still there are lots of misunderstandings regarding Blood Donation. Even so called literate people say if we donate blood our nerves will become weak and who will donate for us during our need, so on and so forth. Eradication of this misunderstanding and educating people regarding the importance of blood donation can be done through NSS volunteers. Even AIDS awareness program can be done through NSS.

- **Communal harmony and eradication of anti social activities:** By doing street plays on communal harmony, we can bring awareness in the society. Regarding eradication of antisocial activity program we have to properly frame and chalk out the activities that can be done through NSS without violating the objectives of NSS.

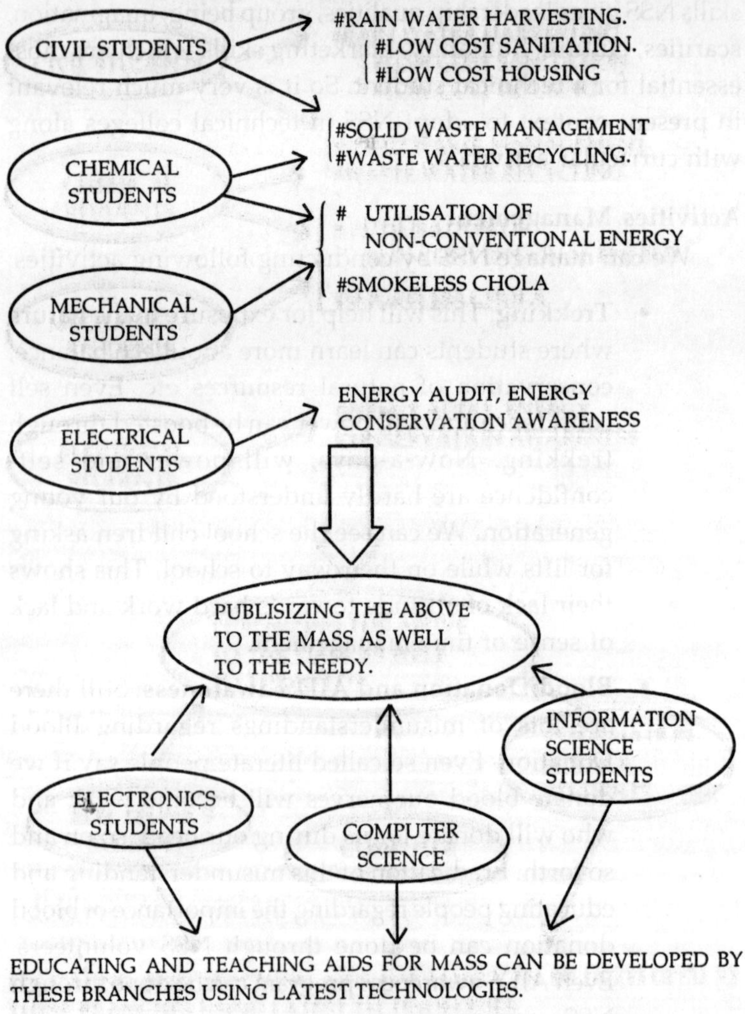

Above are only few general activities that can be done through NSS. In order to suit to our technical colleges we have to redesign the objectives of NSS. Following are some of the activities that can be organized through NSS.

- By providing platform for the students to explore their ideas or inventions for social problems.

Above are few fields in different engineering branches that the students can take up projects through NSS. Initially we can concentrate with in campus only for above said activities.

Implementation and Monitoring

Implementation is one important and serious issue. This can be done only through top authority of the institution. The cycle will not complete until the framed activities are implemented successfully, reviewed and monitored properly. For this responsible team members headed by a senior chairperson is a must. For good conduct of NSS one should have positive attitude.

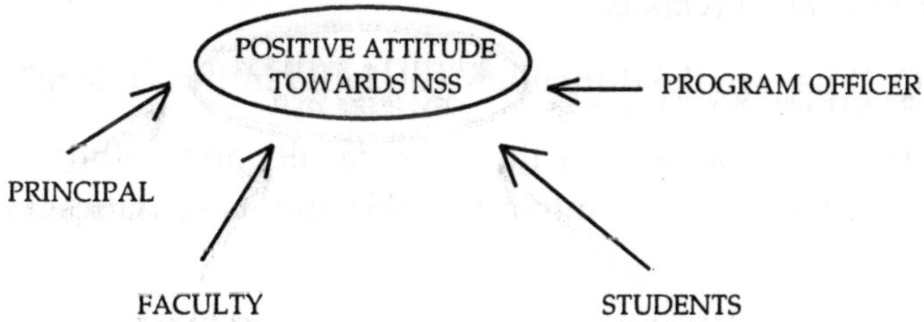

Figure: NSS Team

Conclusions

We can conclude that for technical students NSS is a must, even we can think of doing compulsion as in IIT's it has been already a success story. If there is accountability for this co curricular activity definitely NSS will gain importance in technical colleges.

REFERENCES

- NSS Programme officers training notes.
- Miss Arati R Patrame, Beltangadi, ***"Pattetara Chatuvatikegalege Protsahavirale"***, Taruna Spandana, PP.58 Taranga, July22, 2004 Kannada weekly magazine.
- Dr. Vamanmurthy Kulkarni, **"Hiriya Netara Hardikar"**, PP1, Saptahika Sourabha, Samyukta Karnataka, August 22,2004, Kannada daily newspaper.

DISCUSSIONS

Q: How much it is relevant to make "marketing" as a part of NSS activities?

A: We have done it, only this time, just to give the students an exposure to marketing.

Q: Any credits by government for NSS like NCC?

A: No. It's a service activity. One should not expect returns.

However it can be made a part of curriculum as in Agricultural University.

Q: What are the difficulties you faced in this college?

A: There is a need for the entire faculty and authorities to take more and more interest in NSS and its activities.

24

HOSTEL MANAGEMENT

B. Dinesh Ballullaya
Asst. Prof., E&E Dept.,
S.D.M. College of Engg. & Tech.,
Dharwad- 580002

ABSTRACT

Hostel life is an important period in a student's life, particularly so, if the student is studying in a professional college. Hostel is the place wherein, a student comes in close contact with other students coming from different places, speaking different languages. It is the place where there are ample opportunities to develop one's personality. Life style in hostel plays a major role in the all round development of a student. In this paper, an attempt is made by the author to discuss the problems of hostel management based on his experience as hostel Warden.

Introduction

Hostel for any student is a home away from home. A student desirous of taking admission to a hostel expects to have the following amenities in the hostel: (i) Spacious, well ventilated and furnished room (ii) Good number of clean bathrooms and toilets (iii) Spacious dining hall (iv) Hygienic and healthy food (v) Recreation and sports room to spend leisure time (vi) Clean water for drinking and water cooler (vii) Hot water facility etc. In addition to these facilities students expect to have good conveyance, easy access to STD booth, browsing center, college library, xerox center, medical shop, cafeteria, gymnasium etc. It will definitely be the desire of any student to have a spacious playground by the side of the hostel. A well maintained garden in front of the hostels adds to the beauty of the building. Following are the routine works / responsibilities in hostel management.

Room Allotment

Merit of the student should get the topmost priority while allotting rooms to senior students. In addition, past record of the student like behavior, punctuality in paying mess bill etc. may also be considered. While allotting rooms to first year students, those who come from far off places must be given preference. It is rather a tough job to allot rooms to the satisfaction of all students. Room allotment may be done in the following ways

A. Allotting rooms in serial order as and when a student takes admission to hostel. This procedure is easy and straight forward. However students do not have a choice of rooms or room mates.

B. Giving flexibility to students to select their room as well as roommates .This procedure appears to be the best and could be followed while allotting rooms to senior students. This procedure may not be suitable in case of junior students as they require some time to know each other.

C. Identifying the students hailing from same place/ state and allocate rooms accordingly. This procedure seems to be the best for newly admitted students. Students may be given a chance to change their rooms at a later date on mutual basis.

Once a room is allotted, a student may be permitted to continue in the same room till the completion of the course. However, for administrative reasons, it is better to accommodate the students in separate blocks like 1st year block, 2nd year block etc.

Mess Facility

Major unrest in any hostel is due to mess. If it is transparent, bulk of the problems can be solved. Two options can be thought of:

(i) Assign the work of running the mess to an outside agency. There are two types here. In first type, contractor takes indent from inmates and provides the same. Here, mess bill depends upon the inmate's selection. In the second type, menu will be selected in consultation with the inmates. Mess bill will be a fixed amount. However, hostel authorities do not have much control over the quality of the food served. It may not be possible to cancel the agreement easily in the middle.

(ii) Running the mess on no loss - no profit basis: Mess bill will be on dividing basis, hostel authorities have more freedom. Students can have active participation in deciding the menu and on the purchase process. Here, there is every chance for improvement. Expenses towards mess workers' salary and food may either be met by the students or from the establishment amount.

Discipline

There shall not be any compromise as far as discipline is considered. For every hostel, there must be a set of rules and regulations. Inmates must be educated to follow them strictly. Violation of any rule to the extent of hampering the congenial atmosphere of the hostel should be seriously viewed and parents should be informed about the action taken against their wards .Cooperation of parents should be sought in this regard. Entry of outsiders to the hostels should be strictly monitored. A movement register should be maintained in every hostel to record the movement of inmates and entry of outsiders particularly during odd hours. All efforts must be made to curb ragging in hostels. There should not be any hesitation in punishing the culprits. Senior students need to be educated against the ill effects of ragging and the juniors must be given all the necessary advice and support in this regard. Few get together parties and cultural programs in hostels will definitely help in bringing the senior and junior students together.

Medical Facility

A fully equipped dispensary in the campus will be of great help to face any casualty. If this facility does not exist, a doctor should pay visit to the hostels every day. Regular check up of hostel workers particularly those people who work in kitchen is very much essential. Visit of lady doctor to ladies hostels will be of great help to the inmates. Few lectures could be arranged in the hostels by eminent doctors for the benefit of inmates and workers.

Sports Facility

Sports are very much essential for the overall development of any student. It is well said that healthy body has a healthy mind. Students need to be encouraged to take part in sports events. Inter-hostel competitions may be conducted every year. Hostel should have a sports room so that students can play games like carom, chess, table tennis etc. without disturbing other inmates.

Meetings

At least once in a month, hostel authorities should conduct a meeting with student representatives. Inmates should be taken in to confidence while making decisions. Further, wardens should fix some timing to meet the inmates to know their grievances. This will definitely help in the smooth functioning of hostels.

Data Management

A data base may be created such that once a student is admitted to the hostel, a file may be opened in the name of the student and information about the student such as, room number, permanent address with phone number of parents ,class, roll number, examination number, previous semester results, details of mess bill etc. be made available. Similarly, all information regarding stock, daily transactions, daily issues, student's mess leave details, details of payment made to the vendors etc. should be available at any time.

Hostel Library

Separate conventional and digital library in the hostel will cater to the needs of students, particularly for their project work, internal tests and examinations.

Safety Measures

First aid facility is a must. Yearly once compulsory first aid training against electrical shocks and fire hazards be given. First aid charts have to be displayed for emergency needs. In addition, fire extinguishers are to be installed particularly in kitchen.

Routine Maintenance

Budgetary provision must be made for routine maintenance like white washing and painting, gas pipeline repairs, servicing of kitchen appliances, boiler maintenance, bath room and toilet maintenance and other repair/ replacements. Some works need to be attended immediately and the hostel authorities be given freedom to take decisions in consultation with student representatives and permission of head of the institution may be sought later.

Awareness Programmes

Each student must be properly educated to conserve energy, water inside the hostels. They must be advised to use these resources judiciously. This is indeed an important issue in ladies hostel as girls prepare food inside the rooms and wish to use hot water lavishly as and when they like. Regular supervision will reduce wastage of these resources to a great extent. Today, ETP plants and bio gas plants are gaining their popularity, in addition to solar gadgets to conserve energy. This needs proper education to the inmates to get maximum benefit.

Community Service

Voluntary activities like arranging blood donation camp, donating dress to the poor etc. can be taken up by the hostel inmates. Students should be motivated in this direction.

Welfare of Hostel Workers

It is the duty of the hostel authorities to see that hostel workers are not deprived of basic facilities. Dedicated team of workers is a must for the smooth functioning of hostels. Worker's welfare fund may be established to face any casualties. As a social service, children of hostel workers may be given free primary education in the institutions run by the management and they may be given preference in recruitments at hostels.

Conclusions

Every instant in hostel management involves continuous coordination between inmates, workers, management and finance. It should be transparent to create a congenial atmosphere so that every one feels homely. Though there is a set of rules and regulations to be adhered to, accomplishing cordial relationship amongst inmates, workers and hostel authorities is really an art. Sincere effort and commitment by all the concerned is required in achieving the above goal.

DISCUSSIONS

Q: How to avoid the problem of food – wastage in hostel?

A: Proper education and surprise visits by warden will reduce it.

Q: Is there guest room facility for industry personnel?

A: Yes. However it can be used for short – time stay like relaxing in afternoon.

Q: Has ragging been reduced? Predefined visit-timing of faculty is useful?

A: Yes successfully — due to the cooperation of all the faculty. Though surprise visits are more useful, for more official reasons, scheduling is done.

Q: How about maintaining medical details of each student like blood group, allergy aspects etc.

A: Attempts are on to include such health aspects in each student file.

Suggestion: Put penalty on those who waste food.

THEME E

GENERAL

25

KNOWLEDGE NAVIGATORS

Dr Vinayak Bankapur
Senior Librarian
SDM College of Engg. and Tech.,
Dharwad-580 002

Sunil Mansur
Asst. Librarian
SDM College of Engg. and Tech.,
Dharwad-580 002

ABSTRACT

"Knowledge Explosion" and "Information Explosion" are the terminologies used to represent the growth of Knowledge. Knowledge gets accumulated; the process of organizing knowledge available in different formats is the skilled work of the Knowledge workers. Rendering the services in different formats to the end users is the challenging job of today's world of learning .Librarian or the knowledge navigator's task comprises of application of newer thought, management principles and information technology to develop , diffuse and utilize knowledge. Knowledge Utilized is Knowledge produced. Information tool are designed and developed to help the learning process in the education dissemination system.

Knowledge Utilized is Knowledge Produced
-Bankapur.V

Introduction

Knowledge is power .The 21st Century is the age of

"Information science and technology". Due to the great development of the computer and communication technology, and the fast advancement in communication techniques, the new information and the advanced knowledge are spreading worldwide and penetrating into every part of the world. The growth Knowledge is tremendous. Knowledge organization and management is the need of the hour. Since the advent of the technologies, the recorded knowledge in print and non-print materials has been growing day by day. The electronic media particularly the Internet medium is exploring the access to an every possible Knowledge. The Knowledge Navigators (Librarian /Information Specialist) have a challenge to adapt to the newer technological environment and develop skill to organize the growth of knowledge using different techniques of management science, technology application and developing Knowledge diffusing mechanism.

Growth of Knowledge

Knowledge grows in leaps and bounds. More than 1,600 daily newspapers spew out 62.3 million copies a day in the United States alone. The nation's top 100 magazines produce about 240 million copies per issue. Knowledge grows at such alarming rate.

Timeline for Growth of Knowledge

2002 The Library of Congress collection includes 120 million items

2002 The United States finances 44% of world R&D spending

2001 The U.S. Patent Office has issued a total of over 6 million patents

2001 More than 1,000,000 scientists and engineers work on industrial research and development in the United States

2000 About $265 billion is spent on industrial research and development in the United States

1994 About 50,000 papers are published annually in mathematics

1982 Technical and scientific information doubles every 5.5 years

1982 Over 6,000 scientific articles and 1,000 books are published daily

1978 The Library of Congress collection includes 74 million items

1971 Michael Hart launches the Project Gutenberg digital library

1950 There are 1,000,000 scientists worldwide

1900 There are 100,000 scientists worldwide

1873 Melvil Dewey invents the Dewey Decimal Classification System

1870 About 840 papers are published in mathematics during this year

1850 There are 10,000 scientists worldwide

1836 The U.S. Patent Office has issued a total of about 10,000 patents

1800 There are 1,000 scientists worldwide

1800 The Library of Congress is founded in the United States

1790 The first patent is issued by the U.S. Patent Office

1772 Diderot completes his 28-volume Encyclopedia

1771 The first edition of the Encyclopedia Britannica is published

1500 Approximately 35,000 books have been printed

1455 Johann Gutenburg prints the 42-line Bible

1244 The University of Rome is founded

1231 Cambridge University is founded

1230 Vincent of Beauvais compiles knowledge obtained from translations of Greek and Arabic books

1229 The University of Toulouse is founded

1224 The University of Naples is founded

1222 The University of Padua is founded

1209 Cambridge University is founded

1200 The University of Paris receives its charter

1168 Oxford University is founded

1088 The first European university is founded in Bologna

598 The first school in England is established at Canterbury

370 There are 28 public libraries in Rome

BCE

28 The Octavian and Palantine libraries are established in Rome

39 The first public library is established in Rome

295 The library at Alexandria contains 700,000 manuscripts

335 Aristotle founds the Lyceum

386 Plato founds the Academy

Information Explosion

Today we live in a society that is rapidly changing due to amazing advances in communications and technology. These changes are accompanied by an extreme proliferation of information in both print and electronic formats – what we call it as **"Information Explosion"**. This current "explosion" of information raises new challenges for librarians, because, in supporting the learning and research needs of their parent institutions, they must now contend with an enormous information base in a multitude of formats – graphical, aural, and textual. Not only that, but increasingly, information is coming through in unfiltered formats, which raises questions about the authenticity, credibility, and validity of that information.

Worldwide Production of Printed Original Content, if Stored Digitally in Terabytes Circa 2002. Upper Estimate is Scanned; Lower Estimate is Compressed.

Storage Medium	*Type of Content*	*Terabytes / Yr Upper Estimate*	*Terabytes/ Yr Lower Estimate*	*1999 Upper Estimate*	*1999 Lower Estimate*	*% Change Upper Estimates*
Paper	Books	39	8	39	8	0
	Newspapers	138.4	27.7	124	25	12%
	Office Documents	1,397.5	279.5	975	195	43%
	Mass market periodicals	52	10	52	10	0
	Journals	6	1.3	9	2	-33%
	Newsletters	0.9	0.2	0.8	0.2	0
	Subtotal	**1,633.8**	**326.7**	**1,199.8**	**240.2**	**36%**

Knowledge Centers: Extension of Class Room

Knowledge Centers (Libraries) have traditionally supported self learning and are involved in many national/ regional programs that are being developed to improve learning process. There is encouragement and promotion of reading skills, which provide the foundation for self learning The effective role in the support of learning, knowledge centre need to understand their customers, the learners. They need to know how people learn and how the provision of information and information resources contributes to learning. Customer needs must then be translated into services through a thorough understanding of the changing socio-cultural, economic and educational environment. Services of the Knowledge centers in meeting the challenge of creating an appropriate support to effective learning.. The changing customer base and the changing higher education and library environments require much skills and tactics on the part of the knowledge navigators by using the modern information retrieval tools. The responsibilities of the libraries are

1. to collect the proper information to support the coursework and research needs, and
2. to organize the information materials in a suitable way that makes the information access easily and efficiently.

Role of Knowledge Navigators (Library Specialist)

The transition of traditional library collections to digital or virtual collections presented the librarian with new opportunities. The Internet, Web environment and associated sophisticated tools have given the librarian a new dynamic role to play and serve the new information based society in better ways than hitherto. Because of the powerful features of Web i.e. distributed, heterogeneous, collaborative, multimedia, multi-protocol, hypermedia-oriented architecture, World Wide Web. Possibilities accessing information has in areas such as digital libraries, virtual libraries, scientific information retrieval and dissemination have become easy. Not only the world is becoming interconnected, but also the use of Internet and Web has changed the fundamental roles, paradigms, and organizational culture of libraries and librarians as well.

Today Library Specialist are referred as "Knowledge Specialist", who ave continuously engaged in designing tools and techniques and organizing the knowledge in changing environment . The task involves:

- Organize digital information;
- Disseminate digital information from the computer-held digital content;
- Provide digital reference services and electronic information services;
- Handle the tasks of massive digitization, digital storage process, and digital preservation;
- Provide universal access and retrieval of digital content;
- Catalogue and classify digital documents;
- Maintain the intranet, managing new inputs, user access control, etc.

Tools and Techniques for Knowledge Organization

1. Classification schemes (**Knowledge Organizing System**)
   - Colon classification(CC)
   - Universal Decimal classification(UDC)- Used in BIS
   - Dewey Decimal classification(DDC)- Universally Used in Library
2. Cataloguing (Metadata)
   - Classified catalogue code (CCC)
   - Anglo American Cataloguing Code (AACR)
3. Indexing, INTERCAT
4. Abstracting: (LISA /INSPEC)
5. Thesauri (CAB, INSPEC,)
6. Internet and WWW: Digital Libraries and Virtual
7. Artificial Intelligence (AI) Medical Information Systems
8. Natural language Processing (IR)

9. Concept based searching (IR)
10. Search engines (Google, Rediff.)
11. Automatic summaries: (CITE)
12. Query Expansions (IR)
13. Query by example (IR)
14. Probabilistic Logic (IR)
15. Web Indexing.

7. Navigators Skills

The competency of a librarian is represented by different sets of skills, attitudes and values that enable him/her to work as digital information professional. The following are the skills and competencies required for a librarian.

1. Internet

- Navigation, browsing, and filtering skills;
- Skills in retrieving, accessing required digital documents in time;
- Skills in searching network databases in a number of digital sources and websites;
- Skills in creating home pages, content conversion, downloading techniques;
- Skills in web publishing and electronic publishing;
- Skills in archiving digital documents, locating them;
- Skills in digital preservation and storage techniques;

2. Multimedia and Digital Media Processing

- Multimedia indexing, image processing;
- Interactive digital communications and visualization;
- Cataloguing and classification of digital documents, digital content;

- Searching and retrieval of text, images and other multimedia objects;
- Speech recognition, image visualization technologies;
- Conferencing techniques including teleconferencing.

3. Digital and Online Information Systems

- Development of digital information sources;
- Digitization of print collections(Retro Conversion);
- Competency to manage CD-ROM network station;
- Development of machine readable catalogue records;
- Design and development of databases.

4. Internal Networks

Should be able to develop:

- Personal networks;
- Project teams, competence groups;
- Internal digital knowledge resource;
- Intranets.

5. External Networks

Should be able to develop

- External knowledge resources;
- External personal networks;
- Extranets

Librarians in the Changing Digital Environment

- Librarians As Search Intermediary
- Librarian As Facilitator

- Librarian As Researcher
- Librarians As End-User Trainer/ Educator
- Librarian As Interface Designer
- Librarian as Knowledge manager/professional
- Librarian As Web Site Builder or Publisher
- Librarian As Sifter of Information Resources

The Librarians, whether they work in collection management, reference, or technical services, must take on new roles as knowledge navigators imparting the following duties.

- Knowledge management developers, working more closely with faculty and students to design, organize, and maintain a broader range of digital assets;
- Knowledge management integrators, having a more active role in the educational and research mission of university, integrating information resources and services in course and research projects;
- Knowledge management educators; teaching and training students and faculty information literacy and how to organize, preserve, and share their own information resources;
- Knowledge management researchers, applying library and information science and new digital technology to create new organizational (metadata), retrieval, and storage (preservation) options.

Conclusion

The Knowledge navigator are the link to knowledge. This knowledge disseminations skills are the art developed by them. Designing and developing a system to represent the knowledge in a systematic way is the hidden knowledge of the navigators.

REFERENCES

1. Unesco: How much information. **UNESCO Handbook, 2003.**
2. Fowler, Mary Ann: Knowledge Growth, **LIBR500**, 2003.
3. Jii-Sheng Hsieh and Chia Szu Lo: The role of university Library in Modern Engineering Education **ICEE PROCEEDINGS PAPERS 2000**.
4. Amin, Saiful: Role of Librarian in content Management, **IASLIC SPECIAL CONFERENCE PROCEEDINGS, 2002.**
5. www.innovationwatch .com
6. Bankapur V.M. & Mansur Sunil: Total quality management for Library and Information System. **University News** 39(28) 2001.

DISCUSSIONS

Q: What are the facilities in our library for knowledge navigation?

A: Campus networking is done. Attempts are on to get access to important database.

26

ACTIVE INSTITUTE-INDUSTRY INTERACTION

Girish V. Attimarad
Asst. Professor, Dept. of E&C,
S.D.M. College of Engg. & Tech.,
Dharwad- 580002

ABSTRACT

Active, strong institute-industry relationship is fundamental requirement for the economic growth of a nation. An industry's success depends on the quality of engineering graduates who would eventually work for them. Research provides an important bridge, linking industry and academia. It is the joint responsibility of institution and industry to share a common goal namely improving the competitiveness of industry. Success depends upon partnership in research.

Institute and Industry Relationship

An institute should be dedicated to the advancement of learning through research. As industry is the ultimate customer of engineering graduates, its satisfaction about standards and contents is important. Hence the industry must give continuous feedback to the institutes so as to avoid wastage of time, effort and maintain the need based curricula. Engineering institutes on the other hand must educate the scholars to adopt a new enhanced curriculum which suits the small scale and modern IT industries.

There are many ways in which institution can interact with the industry. The faculty should spend time in industries (during vacations) which will help them gain industrial experience and helps to update the content of engineering curricula. The faculty can adopt new techniques and practical methods to teach the scholars. New technologies will have to go through the stages of research, design, development in the institutions by the faculty and must have a close linkage with industry for the final outcome. The industries are usually keen to undertake continuing education programs for their employees and take advantage of engineering faculties' expertise for conducting specialized courses. During the interactions with the industrial people the faculty can gain the knowledge of practical difficulties in final outcome.

The industries also permit students to visit the industry and provide training. The students must under take their major projects related to the industries' specific requirements under the guidance of teaching faculty. Thus continuing education programs, consultancy, industrial visit and training, sponsored and cooperative research, testing, curriculum revision meetings, student's projects, and well equipped industry oriented laboratories are some of the relevant areas of industry institute interaction. Education and training for the profession of engineering must be related and relevant to the short and long term needs of the modern industry. To ensure relevance, the institute has to continuously monitor the needs of industry and update the laboratories with modern equipments and software.

Conclusion

The active institute industry interaction cell will be one of the effective way to interact with the industries in conducting entrepreneurship programs and consultancy services. The interaction between institution and industry helps the faculty to take industry oriented R&D projects, to design and develop curriculum of the engineering, based on the requirements of the industries. Thus provides value added education for the students. Students in turn get the knowledge of practical courses which they have to study to meet the current trends.

DISCUSSIONS

Q: Whether doing projects in industry is better than doing in college?

A: Yes. Students get better exposure to industrial environment.

Q: VTU has restricted the students from going to industry for the project work, as staff will know little about the work done. Is it not better to send staff for Industrial Training?

A: Yes. It's better.

Q: In some courses, students have to undergo compulsory industrial training. Comment on it.

A: It is a good practice.

27

DRESS CODE AT SDMCET AND A UNIQUE ACTIVITY "FRIDAY-KHADI DAY"

Mrityunjaya Kappali
Asst. Professor, Dept. of E&E Engg.,
S.D.M. College of Engg. & Tech.,
Dharwad- 580002

ABSTRACT

Dress is an important aspect of our day-to-day life. Moreso for result oriented specific objective workplace like engineering college. Evolving proper dress code gives a different image to the people and college. It leads to a mind-set which is more positive and increases the efficiency of the personnel. Present paper discusses about dressing practice at SDMCET. A unique voluntary activity. "Friday – Khadi Day" practiced there since two years, is presented. Finally a simple and effective dress code is proposed.

1. Introduction

Dressing is personality symbolized. It is the way a person is and has to be. Different factors affecting the type of dressing are gender, physique, profession, economic and social status, attitude, weather, living place, companions, religious beliefs, perceptions of obscenity, manners and etiquettes etc. Any one type of dressing will not satisfy all these aspects simultaneously. Hence one has to make a selection satisfying the priority aspects.

Since the factors affecting are too diversified, we find wide variety of dresses. However a little pondering reveals some common patterns of dressing based on locality, profession, religion etc. Such a feature is either a natural happening or intentionally incorporated.

Dressing may be considered to include headwear, neckwear, body clothing and footwear.

2. Necessity of Dress Code

Generalized dress code is a necessity for civilized society. It's not to be taken as an encroachment into one's personal life. Specifically defined dress code is required for work place where many people work together, as a team, for a single cause under a single administrative umbrella like our college. Such a code will help to

(a) Improve effectiveness & involvement in teaching-learning process.

(b) Assure safety and comfort.

(c) Inculcate sense of attachment to the team and to the vision of the college.

(d) Give sense of discipline.

(e) Maintain serene ambience avoiding provoking overtures.

3. Prevailing dress code

There is no exhaustively defined official dress code for the entire college. However some of the practices observed are as below

3.1 Students (Practical Sessions)

I/II Semester:

Khaki Pant-Apron

For higher semesters

Chemical: Khaki Pant-Apron for some laboratories

Civil: Khaki Pant-Apron/Shoes for some laboratories

E&E: White Apron/Shoes

Mechanical: Khaki Pant-Apron/Shoes for most of the laboratories

3.2 Non-teaching Staff

Helpers, skilled workers: Brown Pant-Shirt.

Instructors: Brown Aprons.

3.3 Security Guards

Khaki Pant/Shirt /Belt/Cap/Shoes.

3.4 "Friday-Khadi Day (FKD)" – Unique Activity at SDMCET

"Friday-Khadi Day" is a unique voluntary activity being practiced at SDMCET. In this, every week on Friday, we wear clothes made of Khadi – with men wearing pant-shirt and ladies wearing saree or salwar-kameez. The response from the authorities, colleagues and students was quite positive when the author initiated this activity in the year 2002. Since then the number of persons following this has increased and is now about 5% at college level. (30%Faculty, 5%Non-Teaching Staff, 2.5%Students).

Why Khadi & That Too on Friday?

This activity has nothing to do with politics or any "isms". It promotes positive attitude & has engineering relevance too. We find that commodities like Earth ware, Khadi cloth, mats, footwear etc. are produced by local people in cottage & small-scale industries. They are in a very bad shape due to globalization and fast technology growth. Being weak financially & technologically they are not able to compete with local bigger companies & multinational companies on quality as well as cost. They need support in terms of technology input so that they become competent & work for survival.

We link ourselves with our surrounding people and their technology if we start using their products. This opens possibilities of developing interest in them & at least some competent engineers coming forward voluntarily to improve their existing technology or innovate new ones enabling them to face the competition. Their sales will increase assuring their livelihood. By this, we engineers and engineering college become more socially relevant to the immediate locality and people. Our activity is aimed at such an objective of orienting the engineering professionals to care for the economically & technologically weaker sections.

For our activity, Khadi is chosen symbolically, out of the different local products, as it's easily available and has better visibility.

Friday is chosen specifically because at SDMCET, Friday afternoon is meant for extra and co-curricular activities. There will be seminars/workshops etc. on this day with large gatherings. Hence wearing Khadi on this day gives a good visibility to our practice and effectively spreads our message to many people.

Advantages

(a) Khadi, as a fabric, is healthy and suitable for all seasons. It's easily available and affordable.

(b) Sense of satisfaction will be obtained, as we all are part of a team involved in a positive attitude activity.

(c) By this we engineers and engineering college become more socially relevant to the immediate locality and people.

(d) The activity helps to develop a culture of positive attitude involving simplicity, concern for weak people, in the students who are the would-be citizens of our country.

4. Proposed Dress Code

Main human components in the college are Faculty, Students and Non-teaching staff. Here both theory and practical classes go on. The practical sessions and work involved differ from branch to branch. Generally mechanical and civil practicals involve possibility of mechanical injuries & clothes getting soiled. Whereas chemical practicals involve possibility of chemical injuries and electrical practicals involve possibility of electric shocks. Electronic and computer practicals demand dust free environment. However the conditions for theory classes are almost uniform across the branches. Keeping these aspects in mind, the dress code is prescribed .The details are as below.

4.1 Cap Wear

It's optional. However for health or religious reasons simple and decent caps may be allowed.

4.2 Neckwear

It's optional. When used, it is to be in the form of necktie.

4.3 Footwear

All are to wear shoes with socks.

- *Wearing shoes increases the sense of responsibility.*

4.4 Belt Around Waste

All those wearing pants are to put on belt around their waste providing proper stiffness.

- *Wearing belt improves physical stiffness, which is very*

useful particularly in practical sessions demanding continuous standing for hours together.

4.5 Clothing

The clothes for daily wearing are to be as mentioned below:

(i) **General and for theory class**

Faculty (gents), students (boys)

Pants / Shirts, Dhoti-Jubba, Pyjama-Jubba, T-shirts, Kurta, Coat over shirt.

Faculty (ladies), staff (ladies), students (girls), Office staff (ladies):

Saree-Choli, Salwar-Kmeez, Over Coat, Chudi-Dar-Vail.

(ii) **Non-teaching staff**

Office/library: Clerks & above: same as in (i)

Helpers, skilled workers: Brown Pant-Shirt.

Instructors: Brown Aprons.

Security guards: Khaki Pant / Shirt (tucked in) / Belt / Cap / Shoes.

(iii) **For Practical Classes**: The dress code for faculty remains the same.

For students it's to be Dark Blue pant-light blue apron for all the departments for all the semesters.

- *The student can use the dress in any branch he enters after his II Semester. Practical dress code for the students throughout the college will become uniform.*

(iv) **Prohibited**: Half pants / Bermudas / Sleeveless / any other style or pattern Looking obscene.

- *This helps to maintain decent culture in the campus creating serene ambience avoiding provoking overtures.*

4.6 Friday-Khadi Day

All, except helpers, skilled workers, instructors, security guards and students having practical sessions, are to wear clothes made of Khadi, preferably locally produced, on every Friday. All other conditions will be the same.

- *This activity helps to develop a positive attitude.*

4.7 College Logo Badge

All are to wear a simple college logo badge on their chest with clear visibility. This will be of 3 colors:

Blue	:	Faculty
Red	:	Non Teaching staff
White	:	Students

- *Wearing college logo will instill in all a sense of solidarity and hence will inspire to aim towards the vision of the college.*

4.8 Personal Hygiene

All should maintain proper personal hygiene and keep their dress clean and neat.

4.9 Dress Week

In recent years, students celebrate "dress-week" every year. Here on different days of a particular week, both the boy and girl students of final semester wear differently like "traditional dress, all blue, all pink" etc.

This may be allowed subject to the condition that they will not dress obscenely. They have to take the permission, for the type of dressing they would like to wear, from their corresponding Head of the Department.

5. Conclusion

Dress is an important aspect of our day-to-day life, more so for result oriented specific objective work place like engineering college. Evolving proper dress code gives a different image to the people and college. It leads to a mind set which is more positive and increases the efficiency of the personnel. Present paper discusses about dressing practice at SDMCET. A unique voluntary activity "Friday – Khadi Day" is presented. Finally a simple and effective dress code is proposed.

ACKNOWLEDGEMENT

The author wishes to thank the authorities of SDMCET, colleagues and students for practicing as well as joining hands in propagating the voluntary activity **"Friday-Khadi Day"**.

REFERENCE

M.R.Kappali (1998) "Engineering Curriculum-An Aspect of Immediate Social Relevance" ISTE National Conference, Bangalore.

DISCUSSIONS

Q: How wearing Khadi is relevant to engineering?

A: It encourages linking us, the engineering professionals with the producers, the local cottage/tiny industries. Naturally engineers start caring for them & start thinking about their technology. Contributions at the level of improving/ substituting available technology will start. This is how wearing Khadi starts becoming relevant to engineering.

Q: Charaka – is it not engineering challenge & should it be redesigned?

A: Yes, it is an engineering challenge. It's true that it was meant for "production by mass" & not "mass production".

There should be redesign to improve the quality of output retaining the advantage "production by mass". But the best of our engineering brains have not cared enough for it. Quite interestingly, the very technologies like CNC lathes, Computers, Automation etc. that are supposed to be for mass production, can be employed for this purpose as well.

Q: How wearing Khadi is related to positive attitude?

A: It leads to developing concern for people around and their technology problems. This is a positive attitude.

RESOLUTION

On the request of the author for passing a resolution to wear Khadi on every Friday, the chair sought the consent of the faculty. Majority from gents' side opted for this. The chair ruled that the resolution was passed & requested the lady-staff to cooperate.

28

ISSUES IN STUDENT MOTIVATION

Vasudev K. Parvati
Faculty, E & C Dept.
S.D.M. College of Engg. & Tech.,
Dharwad- 580002

ABSTRACT

This paper deals with some important issues on the important topic of motivation of students. Motivation to learn is defined as the meaningfulness value and benefits of academic tasks to the learner whether they are intrinsically interesting or *not.*

1. What is Motivation?

Psychologists define motivation as a drive from within that guides, activates, and continues behavior over time (Baron, 1998). Either a student learns through intrinsic or extrinsic motivation. There are different strategies for both types that can be used in a classroom. The keys to motivating students are for the teacher to have a positive attitude, acquire the correct instructional skills, and use the motivational techniques wisely. It's a two way process; both the student and teacher must be active players. Any student can be motivated with the correct amount of attention and guidance.

Student motivation naturally has to do with students' desire to participate in the learning process. But it also concerns the reasons or goals that underlie their involvement or noninvolvement in academic activities. Although students may be equally motivated to perform a task, the sources of their motivation may differ.

Why is Motivation Important for Students?

Most students are good students but they can do better, they already know what to do but they are not doing it. What is missing is a spark called motivation. Motivation is important because a person needs to believe in what he is doing and take responsibility for the same. When people accept responsibility for their behavior and actions their attitude towards life becomes positive. They become more productive personally and professionally. Their relationships become better both at home and at work. Life becomes more meaningful and fulfilled.

The rewards of motivation in both tangible and intangible forms are many. Success, financial rewards, reorganization and a better quality of life is the Hallmark of a highly motivated person. For students the immediate benefit of motivation is better academic performance and its consequences.

2. Introduction to Intrinsic and Extrinsic Forms of Motivation

Intrinsic Motivation

Sometimes a student can be fascinated in a subject and are eager to learn more without outside influence or help. This kind of a situation is when there exists a large amount of intrinsic incentive to motivate a child. It is when a student enjoys an aspect of an activity enough to be motivated within. However, topics that are learned in schools today do not arouse children since they find the information useless in their everyday lives (Slavin). The role of personal interest is crucial in a learning situation. It has been proven that a child who is intrinsically motivated tend to make use of strategies that require a larger amount of effort and that allow them to develop more intensely. They prefer tasks of higher levels than an extrinsically motivated child (Lumsden). Internal motivation is longer lasting that external motivation. When students achieve a feeling of satisfaction, learning occurs more successfully. In order to ensure students are intrinsically motivated, teachers must use certain strategies to encourage this type of learning.

Extrinsic Motivation

Opposite of intrinsic motivation is extrinsic motivation. 'This occurs when a student wants to attain a reward or to steer clear of an external punishment (Lumsden). Weaker than intrinsic incentives, some students rely on extrinsic motivation to survive a class. Rewards, expressing clear expectations, and providing clear feedback will all promote this kind of motivation. Educators must be cautious when using extrinsic incentives in learning situations in order not to decrease students' appreciation of the knowledge given.

3. Overall Keys to Motivation

Motivation is possible by using following keys which will give an orientation to one's mental setup.

a. Positive Attitude

The benefits of a positive attitude are as follows

1. increases productivity
2. fosters team work
3. solves problems
4. improves quality
5. breeds loyalty
6. reduces stress
7. makes for a pleasing personality

The following steps can be used for building a positive attitude.

1. To change focus and look for the positive side of everything
2. To make a habit of doing things now
3. To develop a attitude and gratitude
4. To get into a continuous education mode

With such steps it is possible to build a positive attitude towards of all aspects of life and this will be the prime factor in a motivated individual.

b. Use of Motivational Strategies

Capitalize on Students' Existing Needs

Students learn best when incentives for learning in a classroom satisfy their own motives for enrolling in the course. Some of the needs your students may bring to the classroom are the need to learn something in order to complete a particular task or activity, the need to seek new experiences, the need to perfect skills, the need to overcome challenges, the need to become competent, the need to succeed and do well, the need to feel involved and to interact with other people. Satisfying such needs is rewarding in itself, and such rewards sustain learning more effectively than do grades. Design assignments, in-class activities, and discussion questions to address these kinds of needs. (Source: McMillan and Forsyth)

Ask students to analyze what makes their classes more or less "motivating."

Sass asks his classes to recall two recent class periods, one in which they were highly motivated and one in which their motivation was low. Each student makes a list of specific aspects of the two classes that influenced his or her level of motivation, and students then meet in small groups to reach consensus on characteristics that contribute to high and low motivation. In over twenty courses, Sass reports, the same eight characteristics emerge as major contributors to student motivation

1. Instructor's enthusiasm
2. Relevance of the material
3. Organization of the course
4. Appropriate difficulty level of the material
5. Active involvement of students + Variety
6. Rapport between teacher and students
7. Use of appropriate, concrete, and understandable examples

Of the above factors the ones we can focus on are the instructor's enthusiasm and rapport between students and teachers.

c. Incorporating Instructional Behaviors That Motivate Students

The following aspects of instructor's attitude will help greatly in motivating students Hold high but realistic expectations for your students.

Research has shown that a teacher's expectations have a powerful effect on a student's performance. H you act as though you expect your students to be motivated, hardworking, and interested in the course, they are more likely to be so. Set realistic expectations for students when you make assignments, give presentations, conduct discussions, and grade examinations. "Realistic" in this context means that your standards are high enough to motivate students to do their best work but not so high that students will inevitably be frustrated in trying to meet those expectations. To develop the drive to achieve, students need to believe that achievement is possible which means that you need to provide early opportunities for success. (Sources: American Psychological Association, Bligh, Forsyth and McMillan, Lowman).

Tell Students what They Need to Do to Succeed in Your Course

Do not let your students struggle to figure out what is expected of them. Reassure students that they can do well in your course, and tell them exactly what they must do to succeed. Say something to the effect that "H you can handle the examples on these problem sheets, you can pass the exam. People who have trouble with these examples can ask me for extra help." Or instead of saying, "You're way behind," tell the student "Here is one way you could go about learning the material. How can I help you?" (Sources: Cashin; Tiberius)

Strengthen Students' Self-motivation

Avoid messages that reinforce your power as an instructor or that emphasizes extrinsic rewards. Instead of saying, "I require," "you must" or "you should," stress "I think you will find." or "I will be interested in your reaction." (Source: Lowman)

Avoid Creating Intense Competition Among Students

Competition produces anxiety, which can interfere with learning. Reduce students' tendencies to compare themselves to one another. Bligh reports that students are more attentive, display better comprehension, produce more work, and are more favorable to the teaching method when they work cooperatively in groups rather than compete as individuals. Refrain from public criticisms of students' performance and from comments or activities that pit students against each other. (Sources: Eble; Forsyth and McMillan)

Be Enthusiastic about Your Subject

An instructor's enthusiasm is a crucial factor in student

motivation. If you become bored or apathetic, students will too. Typically, an instructor's enthusiasm comes from confidence, excitement about the content and genuine pleasure in teaching.

4. Advantages of Intrinsic Motivation

Does it really matter whether students are primarily intrinsically or extrinsically oriented toward learning? A growing body of evidence suggests that it does. When intrinsically motivated, students tend to employ strategies that demand more effort and that enable them to process information more deeply (Lepper).

J. Condry and J. Chambers found that when students were confronted with complex intellectual tasks, those with an intrinsic orientation used more logical information gathering and decision-making strategies than did students who were extrinsically oriented. Students with an intrinsic orientation also tend to prefer tasks that are moderately challenging, whereas extrinsically oriented students gravitate toward tasks that are low in degree of difficulty. Extrinsically oriented students are inclined to put forth the minimal amount of effort necessary to get the maximal reward (Lepper).

Although every educational activity cannot, and perhaps should not, be intrinsically motivating, these findings suggest that when teachers can capitalize on existing intrinsic motivation, there are several potential benefits.

5. Student Participation in Learning

Although students' motivational histories accompany them into each new classroom setting, it is essential for teachers to view themselves as "ACTIVE SOCIALIZATION AGENTS capable of stimulating...student motivation to learn" (Brophy). Classroom climate is important If students experience the classroom as a caring, supportive place where there is a sense of belonging and everyone is valued and respected, they will tend to participate more fully in the process of learning.

Extrinsic rewards, on the other hand, should be used with caution, for they have the potential for decreasing existing intrinsic motivation.

What takes place in the classroom is critical, but "the classroom is not an island" (Martin Maehr and Carol Midgley). Depending on their degree of congruence with classroom goals and practices, school wide goals either dilute or enhance classroom efforts. To support motivation to learn, school-level policies and practices should stress "learning, task mastery and effort" (Maehr and Midgley) rather than relative performance and competition.

Work From Students' Strengths and Interests

Find out why students are enrolled in your course, how they feel about the subject matter, and what their expectations are. Then try to devise examples, case studies, or assignments that relate the course content to students' interests and experiences. (Sources: Brock, Cashin, Lucas).

When Possible, Let Students have Some Say in Choosing What Will be Studied

Give students options on term papers or other assignments (but not on tests). Let students decide between two locations (or the field trip, or have them select which topics to explore in greater depth. If possible, include optional or alternative units in the course. (Sources: Ames and Ames; Cashin; Forsyth and McMillan; Lowman).

Increase the Difficulty of the Material as the Semester Progresses

Give students opportunities to succeed at the beginning

of the semester. Once students feel they can succeed, you can gradually increase the difficulty level. If assignments and exams include easier and harder questions, every student will have a chance to experience success as well as challenge. (Source: Cashin).

Vary Your Teaching Methods

Variety reawakens students' involvement in the course and their motivation. Break the routine by incorporating a variety of teaching activities and methods in your course: role playing, debates, brainstorming, discussion, demonstrations, case studies, audiovisual presentations, guest speakers, or small group work. (Source: Forsyth and McMillan).

Emphasize Mastery and Learning Rather than Grades

Researchers recommend de-emphasizing grading by eliminating complex systems of credit points; they also advise against trying to use grades to control nonacademic behavior (for example, lowering grades for missed classes) (Forsyth and McMillan; Lowman). Instead, assign ungraded written work stress the personal satisfaction of doing assignments, and help students measure their progress.

Give Students Feedback as Quickly as Possible

Return tests and papers promptly, and reward success publicly and immediately. Give students some indication of how well they have done and how to improve. Rewards can be as simple as saying a student's response was good, with an indication of why it was good, or mentioning the names of contributors: "Cherry's point about pollution really synthesized the ideas we had been discussing. II (Source: Cashin)

Reward Success

Both positive and negative comments influence

motivation, but research consistently indicates that students are more affected by positive feedback and success. Praise builds students self-confidence, competence, and self-esteem. Recognize sincere efforts even if the product is less than stellar. *H* a student's performance is weak, let the student know that you believe he or she can improve and succeed over time. (Sources: Cashin; Lucas)

Be specific When Giving Negative Feedback

Negative feedback is very powerful and can lead to a negative class atmosphere. Whenever you identify a student's weakness, make it clear that your comments relate to a particular task or performance, not to the student as a person. Try to cushion negative comments with a compliment about aspects of the task in which the student succeeded. (Source: Cashin)

Avoid Demeaning Comments

Many students in your class may be anxious about their performance and abilities. Be sensitive to how you phrase your comments and avoid offhand remarks that might prick their feelings of inadequacy.

6. Case Studies

1. 48 students taking a physics course in an university were divided into 3 groups one group consisted of students whose academic performances was much above average and the other 2 groups had either average or below average academic performances in the last 4 semesters.

   Of these 2 groups 1 group was subjected to intense motivational exercises such as positive suggestions, counseling coaching etc. and other group and left study on its own. Over period of time this group of students could perform better than the first group which comprised of self motivated students. This was possible because the self motivation amongst these groups was increase by the motivation factors mention above.

2. In an experiment carried out in a Engineering college it was found that students who had not been able to clear certain papers over several attempts could be made to do so after a series of counseling sessions which was meant to enhance their self motivation. These sessions mainly focused on the mindset change of the students rather than actual coaching in the subject.

Conclusion

In summary, teachers can play a large role in assisting motivation in both intrinsic and extrinsic motivated students through well thought-out strategies. Instructors must realize that their actions and ways of teaching influence the behavior of their students. True, motivation is an internal process, but teachers can still be a major contributor when students have lost a desire to learn. It is important to understand that motivation can only be achieved when more than one strategy is applied in a classroom. Different students have different needs. It is crucial to attack the problem of unmotivated children from various angles. With the right amount of attention, care, and effort any student can be motivated to learn with the aid of actions exercised by their teachers.

29

IN-HOUSE MEDIA IN EDUCATION

Dr. Vinayak Bankapur
Sr. Librarian,
S.D.M. College of Engg. & Tech.,
Dharwad – 580 002

ABSTRACT

Communication is a "Buzz Word". The technique to communicate the message to others is only by transmitting technologies underlying the mass media which made possible "Human Communication" to an infinitely large number of intended audiences. The power inherent in the mass communication from print to non-print medium like press, film, radio and TV are some form of communicative media to inform, to persuade, to educate and to entertain. The role of this media in education is felt essential to develop the art of communication particularly in the age of competition for information representation to reach the targeted audience. The "art of expressions" is "creativity represented "in different forms of disseminating ideas and thoughts. The in-house magazine, newspaper, newsletter and wall magazine are the efforts of education systems to explore the hidden talent of expressions of individuals and create a platform of exhibition.

Introduction

Communication is the "Buzz Word". The Communicating is the art developed by the human beings since man started understanding and wanted to reach his message to other. The earliest forms of known communications were "gestures" and "clay written tablets" etc. The advances in the technological adventures e.g. the Guttenberg's paper printing machine, Marconi's radio, Bell's telephone and Tim Berners-Lee's Internet have all changed the communication methods from verbal to electronic formats. Communicating is to understand better. The power inherent of communication is to inform, to persuade, to educate and to entertain. The art of expression which is to reach the targeted audiences through different forms from print (Newspaper, magazines, Journals, In-house Bulletins) and non print medium (Audio, Radio, Video, TV and Computers). Every medium has role to play to reach the audiences which it intends to reach.

In-house Media

Every organization has a medium to communicate the news about the organization for the benefit of the members of the organization or the public at large in different forms (in print or electronic medium). The medium to communicate may include the following

1. Brochures

A printed manual with all possible details of the organization usually used in promotional activities.

2. Posters

Normally a good piece of Information highlighting the college infrastructure and other details which it intends to highlight with communicative address of the organization (Telephone/Postal Address/fax/WWW) in any size.

3. Newsletter

A periodical which gives information about the activities and events of the organization composed of the following information inputs:

— A periodical publication.

Yearly, half yearly, quarterly, monthly, fortnightly.

- May give information about the events of the organization.
- Cultural events, educational events like seminars, conferences, and personal achievements, Information projects and experiments, Industrial Visits etc., which are part and parcel of the college activities.
- No restriction of number of pages but usually 10 pages may be more than enough.
- A message by the editor, the head of the Institution focusing on current activities will define what the edition intents to disseminate. Example "WE".

The magazines produced in-house disseminate news and activities of SDMCET

4. College Magazine

A College magazine usually is an annual report of the college which also includes the articles or any other form of expressions, infrastructure details of organization and also information of outgoing students.It can be defined as a medium of expressions to highlight the creativity of students. It is composed of

1. Creative forms like
   - Articles and essays (in any language) on any subject (Specific to Generic)
   - Painting
   - Sketches
   - Photographs
   - Cartoons and caricatures
   - Poems

2. Messages of
   — Head of the Organization

   Head of the Institute

   Editorial Team
3. Mission and Vision statements
4. Details of students (usually the outgoing students), successful students in curriculum and extra-curricular activities.
5. Interviews
6. Designing of the magazine to a standard size making it handy volume
7. Medium of presentations: In print form/ In CD forms /Internet edition

5. Wall Magazine

The wall magazine may be a good platform for expression which is normally mounted on the wall in a predominant a place accessible to all staff and students. It exhibits the hidden talent of the students. Usually all departments will try to have their wall magazine. The Wall Magazine may be a e-wall magazine if the same can be accessible on the Network on the campus or the home page or as a screen saver. A wall magazine can be a general one or a subject specialized.

e.g.: 1. Spandana (Kannada) 2. Capture (English)

6. My Experiment with Capture! The Wall Magazine

Capture magazine was designed by the students and staff team and is being published quarterly. The capture is a platform to exhibit the talents of the student's expression in form of feature article, News events, Photo features, Cartoons and caricatures and paintings etc. with a good editorial. It helps the students to communicate in the Journalistic language as represented in the daily newspaper and tabloids. Capture is creating an environment of "Joy of learning and communicating "in an effective manner. "**Creativity is the Mantra of Expressions: The Joy of learning**. 'The smile will be there only if we create space for creativity and give them the opportunity to discover the joy of learning' –APJ Abdul Kalam. The creative expression of the message may be in different forms one would like to express which may be in the form like articles, photography, painting, sketches and cartooning etc. The "Capture" is capturing Joy of learning with creativity of the students at large.

7. Components of the Newspaper

Newspaper is an other communication media. Creativity forms are more noticed in this media. Normally parts of newspaper includes:

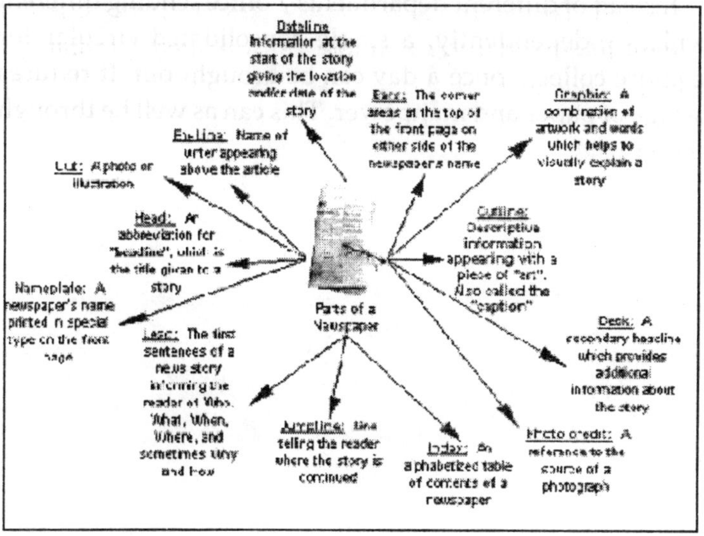

Fig. 1: Part of News Paper

8. Conclusion

Art of expression and communication is the mantra of effective means of transmission of message and knowledge. Technology has helped this inherent quality of communication to the masses in creative representation of ideas and thoughts. Each media has a role to play and a targeted audience. In - house media like brochures, posters, college magazine and wall magazines has intended audience to reach to inform, to persuade, to entertain and to educate.

REFERENCES

(a) Bankapur (VM): World Telecom Day. Reflections, 2000-01. p79

(b) Mala Kumar: Promoting the Joy of Learning. Deccan Herald, 19 Aug. 2004 p.21

(c) Parts of the newspaper : www.east-bue.k12.ia.us.com

Suggestion

Instead of different departments / office sending different circulars independently, a single consolidated circular for the entire college, once a day can be brought out. It reduces wastage of paper and manpower. This can as well be through internet.

30

THE NEED FOR SOCIAL RELEVANCE IN TECHNICAL INSTITUTION

Kiran C. Shindhe
Asst. Professor, Dept. of Mech. Engg.,
S.D.M. College of Engg & Tech.
Dharwad-580 002.
E-mail: kcshindhe@yahoo.com

ABSTRACT

The scenario of technical education has undergone a sea change. The paper discusses some of these issues and highlights the need for focusing on interaction with society, community. A stakeholder analysis is made to identify actors; also the possible interactions are identified with benefits to various actors.

1.0 Introduction

The Indian scenario of technical education, thirty years ago, consisted of a very few engineering colleges, almost all of them aided by the government. Their mission was to cater to the technical needs of the nation with a focus on technology for mass production rather than technology for masses. There was hardly any competition amongst institutions and consequently any need for quality certifying process. The stakeholders of the then technical institution can be shown as below.

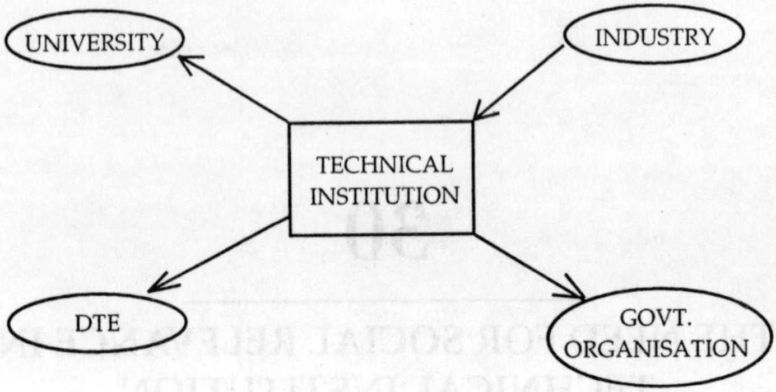

Fig. 1. Stakeholders of a technical institution thirty years ago.

The scenario underwent a radical change when private engineering institutions came into existence mostly in Karnataka state. The globalization resulted in widening of the market for technical graduates both in terms of size and variety of fields. This resulted in extensive development of privately managed technical institutions. The number of institutions increased at a greater rate than the demand for engineers in the country resulting in competition amongst the institutions. The scope of technical education is no longer limited to India but has to cater to global needs. This has highlighted the need for quality certification by National Board of Accreditation and ISO to ensure minimum educational standards. The institutions need to have an edge over their nearest competitor in order to remain in the field. The need for recognition of the institution by the society has become very important for the existence of the institution. This has propelled the privately managed technical institutions to redefine their mission and vision from the viewpoint of the stakeholders.

This stakeholder analysis of an engineering institution shown above helps to identify the various people or organizations towards which the college has a responsibility

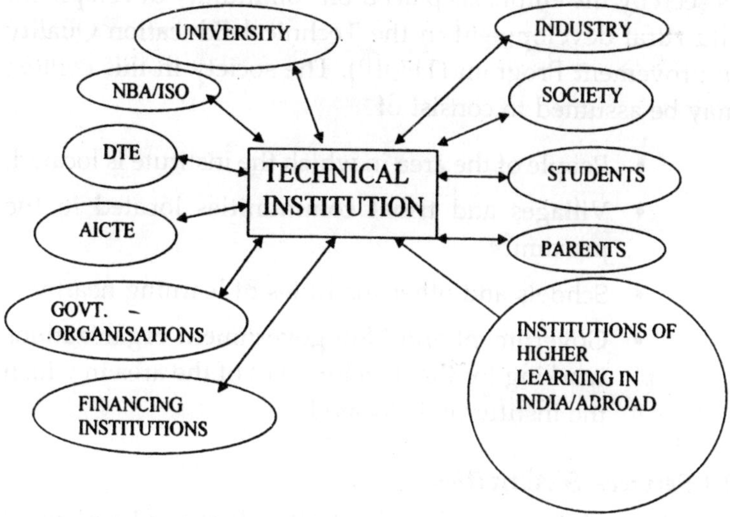

Fig. 2. Stakeholders of technical institution in the current context

or accountability, as they contribute to the existence of the institution. The degree of accountability to stakeholders differs according to the manner in which the institution relates to them. The relationship is decided based upon the management's vision and mission for the institution. It is obvious from the comparison of both stakeholders of a technical institution before thirty years and as on today that the institution has to cater to the needs of greater number of stakeholders for its existence. It can also be seen that the stakeholders on the left hand side have a relationship with the institute, which is more regulatory in nature. Whereas the stakeholders on the right hand side are customers to the institution.

2.0 Social Relevance

The goodwill of an institute is depending on its relationship with society. The government endorses this view as seen by the emphasis placed on community development and rural development in the Technical Education Quality Improvement Program (TEQIP). The society in this context may be assumed to consist of

- People of the area in which the institute is located.
- Villages and tribal communities located in the proximity.
- Schools and other institutes of learning nearby.
- Government and Non-government organizations working for the development of the area in which the institution is located.

2.1 Services & Activities

Some of the services and activities that can be planned within the limitations of the resources of the Institution can be listed as below.

Services to be in the nature of	The activities could be related to
— Improving quality of life — Increasing earnings — Improving employability — Increasing safety — Improving productivity — Improving profitability	— Technical Assistance — Advisory services — Knowledge and skills development/up gradation — Development and/or transfer of technology

The matrix indicates the possible interactions and the linkages that can be developed.

3.0 Benefits

- ***Institution***
  - Recognition, Goodwill, Justification for existence & Payback to Society.
  - Enhanced relevance of technical education to society and economy.

Table 1. Interventions linkages of institutes with surroundings.

	Possible interventions by the Institute				
	Exposure to existing Institutional facilities & Services	*Empowerment by training & Education*	*Addressing Environment, Watershed & Energy Issues*	*Linking Govt. programs*	*Linkages/ Mechanisms*
Schools/Other Learning Institutes	✓	✓			**Institure** Programs
Villages and Tribal Areas	✓	✓	✓	✓	Govt. Programs NGOs and
City of Location	✓	✓	✓	✓	Govt. Programmes NGOs and CBO
Government and NGOs	✓	✓			Institute Programme

- Close linkages with community and industry.
- Development of abilities to form and sustain project teams.
- Improved networking amongst departments.
- Development of competence in faculty and students through solving field problems.
- Internal revenue generation.

- ***Staff & Students***
  - Multi Disciplinary learning.
  - Recognition, Goodwill, Justification for existence & Payback to society.
  - Interaction with development & Government agencies helps understand difficulties for implementation at field level.
  - Satisfaction of seeing the benefits of technology reaching to people.
  - Meaningful Projects.

- ***Society***
  - A dependable institution responding to societal problems.
  - Institution where learning is combined with field level exposure.

4.0 Conclusion

(i) There is a shift in technical education scenario.

(ii) The stakeholders have increased in numbers.

(iii) The globalization has widened the scope and context of technical institutions.

(iv) The Institutes will have to compete globally.

(v) The Institute can no longer be detached from the society and then survive.

(vi) A win –win situation can be created between the Institute and Society.

31

MANAGEMENT ASPECTS IN OVERALL FACULTY DEVELOPMENT

S.G. Joshi
Asst. Professor, Dept. of Civil Engg.
S.D.M. College of Engg. & Tech.
Dharwad-580 002
Email: sgjoshi99@yahoo.com

ABSTRACT

The overall faculty development involves improvement in academic standards (acquiring higher qualification, improvement in results etc.), improvement in financial standards (improvement in monitory income at par with minimum expenditures to be incurred), and improvement in social contacts (public feeling the existence of a guiding personality). All these require proper management aspects including time management, financial management, Resource management etc. In an institution like this, which is celebrating its silver jubilee function, the faculty are having the required skills with rich experience of 15-25 years. But in this supersonic world the only problem is of the time. Some times one may feel 24 hours a day is insufficient. In this context another would like to share a few things about time management and financial management.

Experiment with Water, Sand, Cement and Aggregate

1. Take a glass jar say of 10 Cum. capacity. (Glass jar has been chosen just for its transparent property and we can see what is being put inside the jar.)

2. Put as large size aggregate as possible in to it up to the neck (Say approximately 10 Cum.)
3. Now if you try, small size aggregate can be inserted in to large size aggregate either by pushing or by vibrating. The quantity of such aggregate is say X Cum. (Don't say the jar will break if vibrated. We are doing it in our minds).
4. Now you can pour some amount of sand in to it. Shake the jar it will pierce inside it.
5. Now still you can add some quantity of Cement in to it. Being a fine powder it will readily find some place inside the jar.
6. At last you can pour some quantity of water into the jar.

Remember now you have placed large aggregates, Small aggregates, Sand, Cement and water in to the jar.

Scientifically we can show for producing 10 Cum. of finished 1 2 4 concrete we will be using 15.4 Cum of materials along with 1.6 Cum of water as shown here:

Cement	2.2 Cum
Sand	4.4 Cum
Aggregate	8.8 Cum
Water	1.6 Cum
Total	17.00 Cum

Supposing if you reverse the order of filling—

First fill the jar with water, and if you start filling aggregate, the water starts spilling outside. Supposing if you start filling with sand/cement, aggregates do not find a place inside. That means the reverse procedure of filling up the materials will not hold good and cannot be managed properly.

Now we are relating this analogy to time management

1. It may be lesson planning for a day or for a semester. It can be planning for a carrier or it can be planning for a life time achievement. This will get top priority and we will denote it by large size aggregate.
2. We have other responsibilities also like addressing the students outside the classroom, counseling, family responsibilities like children's education, parents welfare etc. We can not neglect these in our own development/planning activities. This we can denote by small aggregate.
3. There are so many other engagements in life for an individual like social, cultural so on and so forth. This we can denote by sand and cement. (Please note we are not considering the binding property of cement which plays a major role in cement concrete.)
4. And lastly we have our own day-to-day activities like eating, sleeping, entertainment, marketing etc. Like water component in concrete, without which we will not be able to survive.

None of these activities listed above are bad and none of these activities are worth missing. We need activities of the top priority at the same time we need activities that refreshes and relaxes us. Just as the jar has been filled up perfectly by large aggregate, sand, cement and water we need problematic & simple, big & small, heavy & light, tedious & entertaining activities to occupy our lives and the one who can appropriately manage all these can be called as a **PERFECT TIME MANGER.**

Then how about the people who fail in time management and ultimately in work/life? These are the people who start filling the jar in the reverse order i.e. water, cement and sand first and then the aggregate. That means to say they spend most of their time in chatting, browsing, spending time over phone calls of routine nature etc., postponing the important activities of the day to the last moment. They get worried about the work only at the last minute and will not be able to complete it satisfactorily or within time. On the other hand it may take more than the normal routine time because of improper planning.

Supposing if we take up lesson planning, we can do it for a subject for the whole semester or we can do it for a particular one hour duration. If it is for an hour duration in general we can split it in to what is the topic for the hour? Whether it has any linkages to the previous class? Introduction to the topic as such, number of points to be covered, whether it continues to the next class? Is it the end of the topic? And to summarize the topic: There may be differences in categorizing the topics like this because there are subjects of varied nature like some are purely descriptive, some are completely full of numerical, some may have too many sketches to be drawn and explained. Since two subjects carry 100 marks each we can not equate them. The method of handling the subject entirely differs from one another. The time required to cover the same portion differs from person to person. Some times one may stretch the subject beyond limits because of the time duration allotted which may lead to loosing interest in the subject.

I would like to say, time management depends upon the activity to be carried out and the ability of the person to handle the situation.

Coming to the financial management first I must quote here **"A RUPEE SAVED IS A RUPEE EARNED".** Sky is the limit for man's desires. One can think of earning in the right way to the extent possible but then, he should be content with what he has. One can not think of spending Rs.1500/- after earning Rs.1000/- . Then it leads to vicious circle of borrowing and paying penalties. Except for top priority activities like housing, petty loans should be avoided as far as possible. The best way of controlling expenditures is the budget allocation and listing of expenditure. This has many added advantages. One can demarcate unnecessary expenditure and avoid them in future thus getting a grip on financial management.

Small savings is another facet of financial management. In the long run one can build empires by small savings which pile up to huge investments. Small savings will be of much help in case of old age, emergencies and in case of unforeseen heavy health care investments like operations which require heavy amounts in current days.

Finally to conclude, it is said, for completing a given task satisfactorily and within the framework of time, morning hours or first half of the day and first 3-4 days of the week are more productive than the later parts. It is always better to finish off the so called 'heavy' activities when the pool of courage, strength and spirit are overflowing.

You might have heard about the company called 'Packers and Movers". Their slogan is "There should be place for everything and everything should be in its right place". That should be spirit in total management aspects.

Source of inspiration: An article by Shrivatsa Joshi in Vijaya Karnataka, Kannada Daily

32

REFORMS IN ENGINEERING SCHEME AT UNDER GRADUATE LEVEL

Dr. Anand V. Shivapur
Asst. Professor, Dept. of Civil Engg.,
S.D.M. College of Engg. & Tech.,
Dharwad- 580002
E mail: av_shivapur@rediffmail.com

K. V. Pramod
Asst. Professor, Dept. of Civil Engg.,
S.D.M. College of Engg & Tech.,
Dharwad- 580002
E mail: kvpramod2004@yahoo.com

ABSTRACT

Over the years the scheme of education at undergraduate level in engineering has undergone significant changes. Yet, the gap between the need at industry level and institute still exists. In the present paper authors have made an attempt to bring out the deficiency in the existing system and have suggested reform measures to reduce the gap between need and supply. However, greater insight has to be given before application of the proposed system.

Key Words: Education, Industry, scheme, training, subjects.

Introduction

Institutes are known as the temples of learning. These temples should shoulder the responsibility of giving product which are acceptable by the society and industry.

Unfortunately, over the last two decades even though quite a good effort has been put in producing acceptable candidates, still some lacuna exists in the present system. Now, unless we understand and address all the drawbacks that exist in the present system, we may not be able to come out with a tool or a systematic approach in training our students to meet the requirements at industry. Therefore, the system followed in the present scheme has to be reoriented to meet the challenges of tomorrow. In this process it is required to create a platform to deliberate at length the line of work towards making a gap between the demand and supply to a small magnitude.

Why the Examination System?

In any system, whether it is product manufacturing mechanical industry, college or private company, it is required to gauge, either level of understanding or skill depending on the particular situation. So, in case of an institute it is necessary to estimate and understand students' ability to understand and solve the given problem by his/her ability to analyze and solving capacity by the examination or test.

When once he/she goes through such a rigorous test/ examination, it is presumed that the candidate is matured enough to handle the given problem and ability to solve it. In the process of training and aiming at producing end product (Candidate), many a time we as an institute fail to understand the importance of study. Therefore, we end up with a situation that exists in the present scenario. In which students may not be able cope up with the requirement of an employer.

The scheme followed now emphasizes more on theoretical techniques/analysis. Today's world does not require a person with only theoretical skill but also should have communication and other skills, so that he/she can have answer for all the possible questions that may arise during one's service.

Therefore, students should be well prepared with skill and knowledge in a particular discipline so that he/she is accepted as soon as he/she gets a minimum qualification in a particular industry/ company.

Present Scheme

The scheme of education presently consists of eight semesters. In each semester candidate has to appear for few theory and practical examinations in addition to attending internal assessment tests. In the process of learning, students will have to choose few subjects called electives offered to them. The present system gives sufficient scope for choosing the subject from different streams mentioned in the scheme.

The following are some of the main drawbacks in the present system

— Not much liberty is given in selecting subject to come out as an expert at the end of his/her final examination in a particular branch of engineering,

— Students have a tendency to choose a simple and scoring subject at 7 and 8 semester level since their degree is awarded based on their score in these two semesters.

— The elective will be offered only when there are at least 10 candidates in a particular elective subject. Thus some students are compelled to take up electives which are not their true choice.

— The students are more inclined towards securing higher marks than understanding subjects which may help them in the field when they come out of the institute.

— Not much emphasis is laid on training a student to the practical field.

— Present syllabus gives more importance to theoretical skill than a practical exposure.

— No emphasis is given in improving students' ability to improve skill of communication and also analytical thinking.

— In the process of learning, not enough scope exists to participate in extra curricular and sports activities.

Unless a sincere effort is made to fill the gap between what an employer expects from an employee and the kind of training imparted at the undergraduate level, we will not be doing a justice to the society. Therefore curriculum has to be modified as and when time demands to suit to the condition that prevails.

Proposed Scheme

The time has come that we have to train our students in certain specialized courses along with routine courses. In this process we may have to devise a system (Scheme) by which it is possible to bring out students who can best suit to a particular discipline that he/she has chosen. In this connection authors wish to propose the following scheme that will reduce the gap of industry expectation and institute in their opinion.

The first four semesters should be treated as fundamental courses and therefore all subjects which are more or less equally important for all the discipline of the branch should be included. In majority of the branches of engineering the present subjects up to fourth semester can be continued without much change. However small change in one or two subjects may be made based on a specific case. Few of the subjects, that are not really required to be taught, which can be studied by themselves (Self study), may be identified and for such subjects some mechanism of study and evaluation can be thought-of. Authors suggest that such subjects should not be considered to be taught in the class rooms, instead assignments may be given covering the entire syllabus and internal marks may be awarded based on assignments. However, regular examinations by the University should be conducted for such subjects along with other subjects. The fifth and sixth semester subjects should be offered purely based on a particular discipline within the branch. Five subjects in each of the two semesters (5th and 6th) may be specified covering all fields of a particular stream within a branch. It includes theoretical background and understanding of a mechanism of work at industry and site. At seventh semester candidate should be attached to a live project in association with external agency and he/she should gather all information pertaining to his/her work assigned. The collection of information includes going through the journal papers and proceedings on the concerned assignment in addition to collecting information on similar such project taken up earlier or going around in the vicinity of the institute. Seventh semester includes collection of all matters connected to his/her assignments and should present three to four seminars. Seminar should be the criterion for awarding marks for the candidate.

In the final semester candidate has to attend field or official assigned project work under the guidance of supervisor identified prior to the start of the work. Candidate has to forward monthly progress through the industry/office with the comments of the supervisor. At the end of the course, he/she has to submit a copy of the report with the endorsement from the industry/office concerned, to the head of the institute/department. A viva must be conducted for the submitted report as per the practice followed in the present system.

It is equally important to prepare our students for the various competitive examinations which they may have to take to enter into any organization. Hence, there is a need to introduce a comprehensive objective type test at the end of the course. This should be taken as a part of examination system.

If a candidate wishes to have training in another discipline within the branch, after the completion of one's degree, he/ she may be permitted to undergo the course starting from the fifth semester for the new additional degree.

In addition to the suggested schemes authors feel that few of the things may be included by setting aside one of the afternoon slot for training students concerning personality development, group discussion, improving analytical skills, Yoga and other such activities. These programs may be planned through the Dean HR, Training Cell or in consultation with them. During the vacations also, training in professional field may be conducted by the in house faculty or by external experts. These programs will give value addition to their engineering education.

Conclusion

The present system requires certain reforms to be adapted to the rapid change in requirement of the industry/office. The present day demands specialized candidates in their respective field of working environment. Most of the branches of engineering taught today in the various institutions have developed enormously, thanks to the vast research going on, and each branch has got several specialized disciplines within itself. Therefore, the scheme suggested by the authors will help candidates to become experts in particular discipline within a branch making him/her more confident and eligible to be absorbed by the industry/office without need for undergoing any extra training.

DISCUSSIONS

Q: What is appropriate practical – theory ratio? Is it necessary to provide specialization from 5th Sem. onwards?

A: Students can be trained especially in what they are interested, by providing specialization from 5th Sem. onwards.

COMMENTS

In some disciplines it may not be possible to have specialization at the UG level itself. Concept of UG/PG studies should be clear. We should give basic training in any discipline.

33

INVENTION AND INNOVATION AS PART OF CORE ENGINEERING CURRICULUM

V. N. Sukumar
Prof. Dept. of Civil Engg.,
S.D.M. College of Engg. & Tech.,
Dharwad- 580002

ABSTRACT

Technological developments and inventions have been the fuel for growth and development of many civilizations. In recent times also, it was proved beyond doubt that technical breakthrough alone have brought affluence to people of a nation. (1) Our nation is in an unenviable position which dictates that we develop technology to suit our requirements and ambitions. It is clear that many advanced nations do not want to share their expertise with us for several reasons one of them is that our goals are not compatible with their ambitions. In spite of having a large pool of trained man power, we still do not have a system to nurture creativity, spirit of innovation and zeal for invention.

The school curriculum and the ambience which lays emphasis on learning lessons by rote and the system of secondary education which somehow has been reduced to the only task of preparing students to qualify for admission to professional schools are ineffective in inculcating a spirit of enquiry and disinterested curiosity. The only avenue to imbibe students with a sense of scientific pursuit of knowledge and applied research with the goal of contributing to the nation's technological needs is during his/her stay in an institution where he will pursue the goal of acquiring a degree. This presentation will attempt to prove that there is no credence to the established notion that inventors are born, they have a faculty which can not be developed by formal training. Recent studies suggest that a methodology can be developed to direct a student to think in scientific and logical manner which may lead to identification of new avenues for product development. This presentation will cite procedures that can be adopted to orient the human mind towards invention of useful processes, methods and devices.

Introduction

Our country does not have access to some very mundane technological developments. We do not have the know how to further our ambitions in space research and attain self sufficiency in defense related products. At one stage India had to settle for a 27m resolution satellite where as America had already mastered the technology of fabricating and launching satellites with a resolution of 15m. Dr. Kasthurirangan had a poignant point while explaining the reasons for adopting outdated technology. According to him, we learnt the trade based on 27 m resolution satellite to build a better satellite next time.

The developed nations strive to ensure that we do not have access to some established manufacturing techniques like Friction welding, explosive welding etc which are required for our space program. Some of these techniques had to be reinvented (discovered afresh) by our entrepreneurs. We are facing a similar situation in the development of LCA also. Therefore we have to view our LCA project also as a template for an ambitious project to come in the future. Obviously setting our sight on less ambitious goal at the first attempt to learn the basics for implementing a more sophisticated project is most probably the only alternative left for our nation. In fact a long inventory of technologies can be listed which are crucial from national security point of view. A scientific temperament coupled with a specific aim of achieving results can propel our nation towards the goal of self sufficiency in technology in several crucial spheres. Since the nation does not have unlimited resources to commit for research and development, we have to ensure that scientific research and development effort finally leads to inventions which can earn patent rights and are useful to our nation. (Research does not always lead to invention)

***Let us Start the Presentation with a Few Definitions* (2)**

Research

Careful search or enquiry into a subject to discover facts by study or investigation.

The mandate in "Scientific research" is for discovery. Research provides a data base of scientific facts, which means a separate effort is needed to produce something useful. We call that process of adopting scientific knowledge for a specific end use as "applied research". The extreme form of applied research is "Invention".

INVENT v. 1 create by thought; originate (a method, device, etc.).

Invention (n.) 1 Inventing or being invented. 2. Thing invented.

A lot more comprehensive definition can be found in patent laws.

According to The Canadian Patent Act(3) "invention" means any new and useful art, process, machine, manufacture or composition of matter, or any new and useful improvement in any art, process, machine, manufacture or composition of matter;

According to American Patent Law (35 U.S.C. 101 Inventions Patentable.) (4)

Whoever invents or discovers any new and useful process, machine, manufacture, or composition of matter, or any new and useful improvement thereof, may obtain a patent therefore, subject to the conditions and requirements of this title.

(a) The term "invention" means invention or discovery.

(b) The term "process" means process, art, or method, and includes a new use of a known process, machine, manufacture, composition of matter, or material.

Now that we know the definition of invention, let us see why some persons are prolific inventors, where as others do not attempt simple improvisations even in innocuous situations.

Effective inventors tend to display personality characteristics including resourcefulness, resilience, a commitment to practical action, nonconformity, passion for the work, unquenchable optimism, high persistence, high tolerance for complexity and ambiguity, *willingness to delay gratification,* a critical stance toward their own work.

They are able to embrace failure as a learning experience. Successful inventors are self-critical of their own work. They learn to abandon knowledge that may be too constraining. Effective inventors show a range of skills and abilities, including mental flexibility, alertness to problems, opportunities, and deep knowledge.

Some notable aspects of skill include: mental flexibility, alertness to practical problems and opportunities, ability to match one's talents with the problem, using a tool kit of effective ways to conceptualize and break down the problems, and self-knowledge helpful in managing one's endeavors. Characteristically, inventors are deeply knowledgeable about their areas of endeavor, in both a theoretical and "**hands-on**" basis, while comfortable working on the margins of established knowledge.

Many of these traits are characteristics of high performance of almost any sort, and several mark most creative endeavors. A few, such as alertness to practical problems and opportunities and a mix of scientific and hands-on knowledge are fairly specific to invention. To advance their endeavors, inventors commonly need a range of other skills concerned with relating to the constituencies around them. **(Meaning, he should be a generalist)**

Inventors exhibit enormous amount of Disinterested Curiosity about things around them. They lay emphasis on study of the scientific Phenomenon and are capable of perceiving the limitations, deficiencies of the existing system, are mostly unhappy with the systems, gadgets, appliances they use every day. The person is capable of seeing patterns which others may not take cognizance of unless pointed out. Sometimes he is a generalist or at least can appreciate other fields and domains of knowledge. Believes in action and is some kind of a dreamer. Inventors often extend science, pushing the limits of what's understood, finding anomalies in established theories, and disclosing new phenomena that call for scientific explanation.

Successful inventors identify problems and opportunities, isolate important sub-problems, re-frame, re-define, and re-represent problems along the way to an invention. Indices of various kinds of problem finding may be better markers of exceptional *inventiveness than indices of the skill of solving pre-defined problems.* ***(or may be this index should be used to judge intelligence also)(5)***

When we look at the characteristics, traits of an inventor, one cannot but wonder why we cannot train our personality to be discerning in perceiving opportunities and needs for development of new processes, methods, devices etc. One reason could be the acuity many of us have about inventions i.e. we assume that all inventions are the consequence of some earth shattering scientific discovery. But the fact is that most of the inventions are nothing more than a comprehensive, well conceived technical design utilizing already established scientific facts, existing components and circuits, in some extreme cases a new application for an already existing device, equipment or theory. It might be worthwhile enumerating some of the basic traits that govern the evolution of many inventions.

***Characteristics of Invention* (5)**

1. The technological inventions give rise to products that fulfill a need have practical functions in contrast with the products of science ,theories and findings that endeavor to model some fundamental process by factoring out all noise.(utilizing simplifying assumptions to derive an equation to fit the observations)
2. Inventions are not always products and devices but can be algorithms, procedures and processes.
3. Inventions are most of the time useful to the society and are gratefully acknowledged by the populace.
4. Invention has thrived in some societies much more than in others, reflecting the needs and values of the society, and indicating the profound effect of society on inventiveness of individuals and firms.
5. Inventions fill a gap in the need of the society but sometimes an invention is made first and a market is developed later.(Some inventions never find

application ,American patent office has hundreds of patents of this category.)

6. Inventions are sometimes made to serve broad visions like serving the human kind as in medicine, improving communications etc.
7. Sometimes inventions are totally new products and processes, in many instances it is an improvement of an existing product or a totally different product to achieve the same result.
8. The course of invention itself many times leads to better understanding of the phenomenon on which the invention is based because during the course of development several parameters would have been investigated thoroughly and possibly the very frontiers of existing knowledge would have been extensively extrapolated.
9. Many successful inventions are products of extensive experimentations with varying degree of success and frustrating repeated failures. The time frame for the development of a successful product is a function of scientific judgment of the inventor and his erudition in the topic.
10. Luck alone has never been the overriding factor in the evolution of a successful invention. The inventor should be in a position to appreciate the opportunity when it manifests. In Pasteur's well-known phrase, "chance favors the prepared mind."
11. The process of invention intrinsically is not limiting but is constrained by the resources we are willing to commit.
12. Inventions are often modified rather than original, are often a product of absorptive capacity, require focus on window of opportunity and innovation

follows cycles of technological change.

13. Invention is an extended process. The story of any significant invention typically stretches over years (the telephone), decades (the steam engine), and sometimes centuries (the airplane). This extended, complex process contains a rich mix of agents (individuals, groups, teams) engaged in a variety of activities and processes that defy simple, formulaic description.

Cultivating Inventiveness

We have to realize and believe that everyone has the ability to be creative and inventive to some degree and that research shows that such traits and skills can be enhanced.

"very few people make contributions that would be considered technological inventions without intending to make them."

Invention depends on a deep understanding of diverse domains of knowledge of theory, practice, manufacture, fabrication etc.

Having defined the prerequisites for an invention to take place, we can now sset the stage for cultivating INVENTIVENESS

1. Study the existing system, device, equipment, process, methodology.
2. Identify the role, the end result that is expected of the device, process is supposed to perform.
3. Quantify the efficiency, adequacy of the existing system in meeting the goals.
4. Ascertain whether the end user is satisfied with the output.

5. If there is deficiency in performance or dissatisfaction on the part of the end user, then the potential for an alternative device exists.

"Both problem finding and problem solving figure centrally in the process of invention."

The moment a problem is identified we can assume that process of invention has commenced.

The Criteria for Successful Invention (6)

1. There must first be an identified, quantified and accessible market for the invention
2. The problem to be solved (the focus of the inventive activity) must be clearly identified - and there must be an obvious "payoff" that makes a handsome return on the cost of the development.
3. Sound principles of science and engineering must be used throughout "experiments"
4. All the commercial operations of the company must be carefully planned for several years ahead. If the business starts with an ad hoc struggle from one crisis to the next, that struggle will continue indefinitely and the company is likely to fail.
5. The project management must be of a high order, to minimize the cost – and especially to reduce the time - to market the invention.

Phillip Denne, an inventor quotes poet Gray, who was meditating in a churchyard about the isolated lives that had been lived by country folk, whose talents will remain forever unknown. He wrote the immortal line,

"Full many a flower is borne to blush unseen and waste its fragrance on the desert air"

Can Engineering Curriculum Accommodate Requirements to Rrain Students to be Inventors?

There is too much emphasis on working out a range of numerical problems almost to the point of exhausting all available types of numerical examples. The examinations in many instances are of predictable pattern which induces a student to orient his learning towards answering these almost conventional patterns of examinations. So some kind of reorientation is required to inculcate students to be discerning. The emphasis should be on acquisition of knowledge and deeper understanding of the phenomenon. His ability to perceive patterns in seemingly dissimilar processes, identify parallels in different streams of science, finding new applications for existing equipment and processes should be nurtured.

Profile of an Inventor : Phillip Denne (7)

He began his career as physicist and electronics engineer, working on audio and radio-frequency systems before moving into industrial control and a wide range of "Mechatronics". He is well known as an entrepreneur and is the author of over a hundred patents and patent applications. He is especially recognized for his creation of the entertainment simulator and is a world authority on simulator motion systems.

His creations are :

First Telephone Answering Machine

Optimometer for monitoring the adequacy of air / fuel for an oil fired boiler for a power plant.

Simulator for SST (concorde)

Control system to regulate valve to control water in the slurry in a cement plant.

Electronic controls for the first model automatic petrol pump.

His inventions spanned dairy industry, electronic warfare simulator, simulators for entertainment, electromagnetic rams, fire suppression devices, vehicle suspension, and video games and many more areas.

Conclusions

Invention is not a trait which cannot be developed by any reasonably intelligent person. A training program can be devised with emphasis on appreciation of basic principles and a systematic study of existing devices to identify "problem" to invest research efforts. The engineering curriculum can be adopted to cultivate skills required to be inventive. Inventions are not governed by luck alone but depend on the effort that is expended though serendipity has in some cases has proved to be providential.

REFERENCES

1. Entrepreneurship, Innovation and Growth-T. N. Srinivasan Samuel C. Park, Jr. Professor of Economics, Yale University, New Haven, CT USA.
2. Oxford dictionary
3. Patent Law Primer-copyright 1997-2004 *Donald M. Cameron, Ogilvy Renault*
4. Appendix L Patent Laws-United States Code Title 35 - Patents
5. "THE ARCHITECTURE OF INVENTION"THE LEMELSON-MIT PROGRAM School of Engineering Massachusetts Institute of Technology
6. The Children of Necessity Friday evening Discourse to the Royal Institution Feb 23rd 2001, Eur.Ing. Phillip Denne B.Sc. C.Eng. C.Phys. M.Inst.P. F.I.E.E. F.R.I

7. Commercialization of Research Results in the United States- An Overview of Federal and Academic Technology Transfer-A Report Commissioned by the Swedish Ministry of Education and Science-U2001/4567/F-Magnus Karlsson-Science and Technology Attaché-Swedish Institute for Growth Policy Studies, ITPS-Embassy of Sweden, Washington, DC.

34

TODAY'S ENGINEER: A PLAYER IN A GLOBAL MARKET

Nitin Kulkarni
Faculty, Dept. of Mech. Engg.
& Placement Officer,
SDM College of Engg. and Tech.,
Dharwad-580 002

ABSTRACT

Today's fresh engineers are facing a world full of competition. The irony is that they will not be about clear the expectations from their prospective employers. The present paper deals with this aspect. The current scenario regarding selection for employment, expectations from students, action plans by the institutes to improve their students etc. are dealt with.

Introduction

As old as any other profession of the world, Engineering has come itself again at the crossroads. The recent rebound in IT related manpower needs together with the raising monitory benefits; today's fresh engineer is facing truly a world full of chaos. The struggle to define once own position begins even before they complete half of their foundation education in engineering.

The world is changing, especially true for an Indian engineer. At one side, the IT companies beacon him/ her to lure into their folds, at the other end it is the innate desire to be a non computer related engineer like Mechanical, Civil and so on. The world for an engineer is full of competition in which many a times he /she has to play without even knowing the rules of the games. By the time the rules are made known, the competition is over.

Current Scenario

It is truly the survival of the fittest out there especially considering the market sensitivity for a fresh engineer. The number of colleges offering engineering degree has gone multifold each with their own value criterion to boast. Engineers are being churned out at a pace never seen before. Are all these engineers employable? How the companies see them to be fit for their requirements? What are the measuring yardsticks? When companies HR Managers keep expecting an overall developed engineer, how would they measure and how our graduates stand up to it?

Most of the companies would like to have the best in class graduates by the least expensive and less taxing process. Hence proximity of engineering institutions to these Industries does have its own bearing on the number of campus interview a given institution can have. Travel conveniences, connection by Air, train and roads substantially influence ones decision to reach out to farthest colleges. Hence a few initial successes with campus interviews where credibility of the students and in turn that of the institution is sort of put to test.

All along, the HR managers have been curious to know how educated the students are about their company. This also includes awareness regarding the General Management, Products, Technologies, Business practices and such. A student with a good understating of the company information sure will have an edge over others especially during the final interviews. Teaching staff and their qualification, input quality of students can be a crucial decision making criteria for Industries. Better industry – Institute relations can alleviate many of these concerns. This is where the consulting projects undertaken by the teaching staff with industry comes in very handy. Students of that institute not only will have updates on Projects, Technology and such of that company but also generates a favorable environment, which ensures higher student 'hit' rates in job interviews.

Setting Expectations

If we now turn our focus on to the first year student-to-be or a 12th std. Pass-out, matching expectations of the student, Institute and the Industry play a major role. Many of the students are in tuned to be an engineer. Likewise a great deal of them would embrace engineering by peer, family pressure. Based on their CET ranking they get to pick a seat in any given discipline. If for some reason, it is not the college of student's choice, many of the students suffer from immediate to long term depression. Constant handholding, pep talk and gaining maturity levels sometimes help.

Typical students' expectations are, to acquire Skills, Knowledge, and Attitude, improvise analytical, logical skills, language, verbal and written communications, Entrepreneurial skills, excelling under pressure and under competition. The most prominent one of all these and as per many of the HR' Managers visiting our college, is the clarity of communication in English. In today's fast changing world, one has a very small window of opportunity to make an impact and communicating powerfully and effectively is one such tool to make a lasting impression. Better coherence of ideas, thoughts and feelings and expressing them effectively is critical. Till the students faces a real campus interview, viva-voce situation with an external examiner is the only one which comes very close to being an effective simulator for the interview.

Encouraging students to speak in English, making them

read English newspapers and magazines, encouraging students to be a part of interactive class rooms can improve verbal power and effective communication. After few initial rounds of such sessions, most of the students enjoy the 'freedom' they get from talking fluently and openly with strangers. It was a surprising revelation to see students who are good in inter-collegiate debate competition, failed to be effective in Group discussions. Typically students with 4-6 sessions of Group discussion can remarkably transform themselves when actual GD hits them.

If one looks at today's selection procedure for various IT companies, it looks more of a rejection procedure; only a student with multi faceted personality is designed to win. One-to-many (written test) and one-to-few (Group discussion) and one-on-one (personal interview) situation would not let anybody selected if they are not worthy of it. Measurement benchmarks may vary from company to company, but the requirements still calls for an all round achiever. Students' must be enlightened about this.

Students who are introverts can be made to realize their strengths, which they can bank on. A self-analysis by the individual students helps them to focus on the industry of their choice. There are incidents where in software companies prefer a good Engineer only. As long as he or she can present the logic, algorithm effectively across the table, no further enquiry is made into their other "soft skills". Students would not only have to be technically strong and focused, they still need good verbal and written communication skill to be an effective presenter of technical matters across the table.

Action Plans

Based on the understanding of how students think, behave and respond, institutions can take up many activities aimed at helping their graduates be successful in the job market.

1. Imparting Technical knowledge: The effort here should be to enhance the conceptualization skills, so the students can interpret "why" things are done the way they are and not "how". Few ideas to promote such way of thinking are, encouraging students to ask question in their classrooms, having them to prepare and present a chapter or a sub-chapter in academics to the entire class.
2. Cross discipline training: Especially true of computer skills like C and C++ programming for E&C, E&E and Mechanical disciplines. They must be independently able to assess the problem, draw the flowchart, and come up with the logic to solve the problem and finally writing the code.
3. A industry/ sector based knowledge bank: which is created and maintained by students puts them in touch with what to expect in future. This info must include the Organizational structure, Products, Technologies, Customers, Competition, Hiring patterns, Selection procedure Financials etc. This knowledge base must be updated regularly.
4. Preparation of question banks of variety of subjects like General Aptitude, Programming, Analytical skills, Language Logic Puzzles etc.
5. Having students participate in, group discussion on a weekly basis and making participation mandatory. The staff of two can manage the show with precise feedback on the individual performance. Non-participating students who are actually watching the GD give better comments and feedbacks also. A standard list of Do's and Don'ts can be generated which can be passed on to reduce the learning curve.

6. Mock interviews with participation from all involved will be a big booster for the self-confidence. Typical questions asked during the HR rounds can be posed to the individuals and / or to the group. This not only helps students to improve the communication skills, it alleviates the stage fear, improves information on general subjects and prompts them to do better next time.
7. Having a written aptitude test like once in a week with participation from all the students is also one more way of making their analytical skills go up. Having a prize for the best performers will boost the morale and keeps the attendance high.

Action Items on Industry Interactions

1. Understanding of what companies are looking for in our students / graduates. Making students aware of these requirements. Incorporating these requirements while training students of that individual discipline.
2. Inviting individuals in the field of HR or relevant technologies for campus presentations.
3. Coming up with a striking value proposition for the companies as to why "our" students are better, despite them having to travel a long distance to conduct campus interviews. This value proposition must be the collective outcome of all the staff and management.
4. Staff participating in Industry consulting projects, getting results and gaining credibility for the self and the institution.
5. Joint projects with Industry where students and staff can participate and work for a common goal.

REFERENCE

"Strengthening the human resources" Foundation of the Indian IT enabled services/ IT Industry: Report by KPMG in Association with NASCOM.

DISCUSSIONS

Q: Is it not necessary to try for better quality of students at intake stage?

A: Yes it's necessary. Attempts are on towards this.

Q: What are placement facilities for PG students?

A: Somehow that segment is not very much cared for. It will be set right.

Q: Recruitments are happening only in few branches. What about other branches?

A: All the departments are to be represented by a suitable faculty for placement to tackle such problems.

Q: Due to recent recruitments, the number of students going for higher studies has come down. Comment.

A: We can't force students regarding job or higher studies. It's their choice ultimately.

35

TECHNOLOGY IN ANCIENT INDIA

S.B. Karajgi
Asst. Prof. Dept. of E&E,
S.D.M. College of Engg. & Tech.,
Dharwad- 580002
Email: sbkarajgi@hotmail.com

ABSTRACT

This paper deals with technology of ancient India. Studies made in this regard showed that India was well developed in technology during the Vedic period. Efforts are made in this work to collect and consolidate information about these developments.

Introduction

It is known from the history many civilizations existed in the past. These civilizations have seen lots of ups and downs. Some outstanding civilizations survive the ravages of time and continue to exist. Although the glorious part become only a part of history, some salient points still remain and continue to give glimpses of forgotten glory.

The civilization of India is a classic instance. History shows that it once was at the peak but now only the glimpses remain. Even though it is tottering (because of western impact), its vigor and vitality that have sustained it for ages do not allow it to die a sudden inglorious death.

The civilization of India is the earliest and oldest. It is

most dynamic, inherently durable. Many philosophers from all over the world have opined the same.

It is to be noted that India's contribution in the field of medicine and surgery are most phenomenal. Its contribution to mathematics is unforgettable. The importance of the creation of the zero mark can never be exaggerated. Some mathematicians opine that the Hindu adopted the decimal scale very early. The ancient Hindus succeeded with ten signs to express any number in a simple way. This attracted the attention of all civilized people of the world and they adopted that.

The very fact that Indian Science of Astronomy involving precision mathematics, predicted correctly the occurrence of eclipses and other related matters precisely prove this.

Concept of Time

Our ancestors had a wonderful concept of time, shown below.

Brahma's one day	—	Two Kalpas
One Kalpa	—	14 Manvantaras
One Manvantara	—	71 Mahayugas
One Mahayuga	—	Kritayuga,Tretayuga, Dwaparayuga and Kaliyuga
Krita Yuga	—	17, 28,000 years
Treta Yuga	—	12, 96,000 years
Dwapara Yuga	—	8, 64,000 years
Kaliyyuga	—	4, 32,000 years

i.e. Brahma's one day à 858,81,60,000 years

Brahma's one year à 3.1346784×10^{12} years

Life time of Brahma – 100 years à $3.13.46784 \times 10^{14}$ years

According to most of Panchangas, present Brahma has completed 50 years of life.

He is running first day of first month of 51st year.

Already 6 manvantaras are completed – Swayanbhuva, Swarochisha, Uttama, Tapasa, Raivata and Chakshusha.

We are now in 7th Manvantara – Vaivaswata

In that – already 27 Mahayuga's are over. 28th Mahayuga is running and in that, already 38, 88,000 years are completed i.e. Krita, Treta, Dwapara Yugas are over and Kaliyuga has started. In this Kaliyuga, already 5105 years are completed and 4, 26,985 years are remaining.

Though the exact details are <u>left to the belief of individuals</u>, the concept of time which our ancestors had is amazing. However the numbers and the mutual relations appear to be more realistic.

Aeronautics

One would be astounded to know that aeronautics was so developed in India millenniums ago that it had reached almost peak. The oldest records of India – Vedas speak of an aerial navigation. The Ramayana, the Mahabharata, the Bhagavata and others speak of aerial navigation.

It is indeed unknown to many people that sage Bharadwaja wrote an outstanding book on technology – 'Yantra Sarvaswa' which contains 40 sections. Vaimanika Shastra is the most important of all. This section consists of 8 chapters, 100 topics and 500 sutras. There is a commentary on this by Swamy Bodhananda known as Bodhananda Vritti.

Sage Bharadwaja refers, in his Vaimanika Shastra, to other sages – Narayanmuni, Shaunaka, Garga, Vachaspati, Chakrayani and Dhundinatha, who have written books on aeronautics. It means that there were many Rishis who were conversant with technology and who used it.

According to Sage Bharadwaja there were three sorts of

Vimana's – Shakuna Vimana, Rukma Vimana and Sundara Vimana. They were also classified as Mantrik, Tantrik and Yantrik. The last class is more interesting to us. This class of planes was highly perfected.

The aerial paths were five – Rekhapatha, Mandala, Kaksya, Shakti and Kendra. There were military planes beside luxury and commercial ones. It appears that electricity was used for plying the Vimana. They were necessarily equipped with all protective and useful machinery. They were provided with some destructive missiles. There were some machines similar to our modern x ray – known as Guhugarbhadarsha Yantra. The speed of planes ranged from 1000 miles per hour to 20000 miles per hour. Therefore the planes were manufactured from lighter materials. The properties of these materials are mentioned in Lohatatva prakarna. It appears that they had studied magnetism, chemistry, sand, light, electricity, aeronautics etc. Sage Bharadwaja also wrote Amshubodhini –which deals with solar rays.

There are 32 technical secrets which form the background of aeronautical science. Some of these are

- art of manufacturing aeroplanes which are unbreakable, non combustible and indestructible.
- *—vimanastambnana kriyarahasyam"*

  Bringing the fastest moving plane to dead stop quickly.
- Capacity and technical skill to hear conversations, talks, whispers that take place in enemies plane.

  Paravimaanastha janasambhashanadi sarvashabdakarshanarahasyam
- Capacity and technical skill to see and to photograph and televise things, persons, incidents from enemies' plane.

Paravimaanastha vasturoopakarshanarahasyam

- Selection of clothes.
- Diet.
- The materials used in construction.
- Working of motors and generators.
  - — It appears that electricity was generated, using solar energy using a specific 'Mani'. Electric wires were used which were known as Tantri they were covered with 5 kinds of leather.

Aasanaartham draavakaanaam tantreenam veshthanayacha

Panchacharmani shastreshu proktani jnanavith-thamaihi

Charmavoshthita tantribhihi vidyuchchaktiprasaaranam

And many more.

Conclusion

It is really painful to know that full literature for all the above is not available. With whatever little literature we have today, we are not in a position to say technically that these were in existence. However if detailed research is conducted in this direction, we may unearth some useful information.

Edward.P.Rice, a philosopher mentions "No section of the population of India can afford to neglect her ancient heritage. The treasures of knowledge, wisdom and beauty which India contains are too precious to be lost. Every citizen needs to use them if he is to be cultured modern Indian."

In my opinion therefore, as teachers, we make efforts to know about these points and pass on to our next generation so that they will have a glimpse of our great Indian civilization.

36

IMPORTANCE OF PHYSICAL FITNESS

G.L. Rajabanshi
Asst. Prof., Dept. of Mech. Engg.,
S.D.M. College of Engg. & Tech.,
Dharwad – 580 002
Email: rajabansi@yahoo.com

ABSTRACT

Physical fitness is one's richest possession; it cannot be purchased, it has to be earned through a daily routine of physical exercises. The advantages of being physically fit extends from physical, social, economical to as far as psychological gains. The presentation covers the above topics, methods of achieving and maintaining the physical fitness and the possible losses if it is not pursued.

Introduction

It is a proven fact that fit citizens are nation's best assets and weak ones, its liabilities. It is therefore very important to develop awareness for the same among the citizens. It a person's body is underdeveloped or grows soft or inactive and if he/she fails to develop physical prowess, he is undermining his capacity for thought and for work, which are of vital importance to one's own life and society in a welfare state.

There have been continuous attempts by WHO (World Health Organization) to develop awareness among the people, the effort has been backed by IOC (International Olympic Committee).

On the national scenario, Indian Government has taken up this task through programs at various levels throughout the country.

Basis Qualities of Physical Fitness

1. **Cardio-respiratory Endurance:** This is the quality that enables one to continue engaging in reasonably vigorous activities for extended periods of time.
2. **Muscular Endurance:** Enables a person to sustain localized muscle group activities for extended period of time.
3. **Strength:** It is the amount of muscular force one is capable of exerting in a single muscular contraction.
4. **Speed:** It is the ability to make rapid movements of the same type in the shortest possible time.
5. **Power:** It is the quality of muscle to contract forcefully in the quickest possible time.
6. **Agility:** It is the agility of a person to change the direction quickly and effectively.
7. **Flexibility:** It is the functional capacity of a joint to move through a normal range of motion.

Systems Related to Physical Fitness

1. **Skeletal System:** Skeleton serves the body in three ways; protection, support and movements along with muscles. The last two are basis to physical fitness.
2. **Muscular System:** A muscle is an organ made up of bundles of contractile tissues by which movements are brought about. There are three types of muscles in the human body, viz. skeletal muscles, smooth (involuntary or plane), and the cardiac muscle. If the skeletal muscles are properly developed, an efficient movement is possible.

3. **Circulo-respiratory system:** The cardio-respiratory fitness is an important aspect of physical fitness, which is dependent on the efficient working of circulo-respiratory system supplying an adequate amount of oxygen based on exercise demands.
4. **Nervous System:** Is the main system of control of body. Entire body movements take place after receiving impulses from the nervous system. The range of contraction of various muscles is directly related to the strength of nervous system.

Development of Physical Fitness

Regular physical activity is required for an individual to develop and maintain physical fitness. Proper development and maintenance of physical fitness demands a deeper understanding that controls the building up of different components of physical fitness. The principles are

1. **Regularity:** Physical exercises are to be done on regular basis. It is a biological necessity.
2. **Progression:** The extent of physical exercises should be progressively increased to guarantee the physical fitness of a person.
3. **Total body involvement:** The physical exercises program should be designed in such a way that every part of the body is involved in the exercise.
4. **Specificity:** The exercise program must be specific to intended result e.g. speed attainment, power attainment, general fitness etc.
5. **Tolerance:** Every individual has different level of capacity to take the intensity of exercises. The program should be devised keeping this aspect in mind.
6. **Warming up:** The warming up exercises should

be done before actually starting the exercise program this prevents soreness and muscle injury.

7. **Limbering down:** Just as the body needs warming up, it also needs gradual cooling down after the exercise.
8. **Rest and Sleep:** Adequate amount of rest and sleep are vital for regular participation in a physical fitness exercise. Insufficient rest and sleep result in fatigue and adversely affect regularity of the program.

Exercise Programmes

Varieties of exercise programs are enumerated below. Individuals should adopt any one or more, depending upon the need, time, purpose and facilities available.

1. **Callisthenics:** A variety of callisthenics exercises have been developed involving free hand exercises and with apparatus. The selection of exercise program depends, as said, on the purpose, need, time and available facilities. It is recommended that, exercises involving big muscles must be selected in all the programs.
2. **Jogging**
3. **Swimming**
4. **Skipping**
5. **Weight training**
6. **Sports**
7. **Cycling**
8. **Yoga**

Nutrition for Fitness

It is extremely important that a proper balance should be maintained between the intake of food and daily energy expenditure in order to control and maintain ideal body weight.

A well balanced diet should be maintained involving the following components and "AVOID USING YOUR BELLY AS A DUST BIN".

An ideal weight chart for Indian males and females is provided below.

NUTRITION FOR FITNESS

Weight Chart for Indian Women

Wrist Circumference		*Below 13.9 cm (5½ inches)*	*14-16.4 cm (5½ - 6½ in)*	*16.5+ cm (6½ + inches)*
Height Ft.	*In.*	*Small frame Kg.*	*Medium frame Kg.*	*large frame Kg.*
4	7	37	41	45
4	8	38	43	46
4	9	39	44	48
4	10	40	45	50
4	11	42	46	51
5	0	43	48	53
5	1	44	49	54
5	2	45	50	56
5	3	47	52	58
5	4	48	54	60
5	5	50	56	62
5	6	51	58	63
5	7	53	60	65
5	8	55	62	67
5	9	57	63	69
5	10	58	65	71

Evaluation of Physical Fitness

Researches carried out on the physical fitness reveal

following parameters, which can be taken as 'Measure' of physical fitness.

Adult Males

Grading	*Bent Knee Sit-ups (60 sec) (No.)*	*9-Minute Run/Walk (Mts.)*
Very Good	20	1600
Good	16	1400
Average	12	1200
Poor	8	1000
Very Poor	4	800

Adult Female

Grading	*Bent Knee Sit-ups (60 sec) (No.)*	*9-Minute Run/Walk (Mts.)*
Very Good	15	1000
Good	12	900
Average	9	800
Poor	6	700
Very Poor	3	600

Values of Physical Fitness

1. Efficiency in work and performance.
2. Resistance to disease.
3. Efficient functioning of various systems of the body.
4. Longevity.
5. Proportionate development of body.
6. Mental health and Alertness.
7. Preparedness for emergency.
8. Success in games and sports.

Conclusion

Physical fitness is absolutely important for a person. It should be pursued with passion.

REFERENCES

1. Physical fitness-How to develop Dr. A.K. Uppal, Friends publication.
2. Internet sources.

37

ADMINISTRATION AND ORGANIZATION OF SPORTS AT COLLEGE LEVEL

Dr. A.G. Bujurke
Director of Physical Education
S.D.M. College of Engg. & Tech.,
Dharwad-580 002

ABSTRACT

Sports infrastructure, are very important facility. Physical Education plays a major role in sports development in education system particularly the fitness level, training and the moral of the Sports persons. Administrating and managing them with application of latest technology and training facilities will help to get better out put and fare in the competition with confidence. Physical Education teachers are architects, who can mould the talents and fitness of the sports persons and prepare them to compete at National and International level.

1. Introduction

"Sports" is defined as the playing of games or participation in competitive pastime involving physical exertion and skill. Today sports have become more professional and big games have been played across the world. The need for to train the sports person are challenging task of the Physical Education system. To be more efficient, knowledge of the latest skills of the sports management has become very necessary. Sports administration is not only responsible for effective management but also to promote moral standards of sports persons. With the changing scenario of sports world wide sports administrators are to restructure the system to suit the new generation of sports persons. Technological advancements the Hi-Tech equipment are available which are needed for the training and developing of the sports persons. Physical Education teachers are the real architects of sports in the colleges and education institutes. To improve fitness level (which is players very low) and excellence in sports, formation of sports clubs in all games is required.

2. Sports Administration & Management

Sports administration has become a very complex subject these days. Sports administration is not only responsible for effective management but it has also to promote moral standards of sports persons. Sports in education system, if are to be more efficient, they should have the knowledge of latest skills of sports management. Sports management is an art of getting better output from the sports man power.

Sports management requires better interaction with people. With the changing scenario of sports world wide sports administrators are to restructure the system to suit the new generation of sports persons. For better administration of college sports it needs thorough understanding of its various ramifications.

3. Nurseries of Sports Person

Colleges and universities are the nurseries of sports persons. These nurseries must be developed further with utmost care. Many good international players have come from colleges universities. Players do not get required exposure in the national and international competitions. Maximum number of combined university/college teams should participate in the senior national and world university games.

It will give good chance to the young university players to experience better competition at national and international level such type of competition will develop confidence and skill among them.

4. Sports Facilities

In the new century we shall experience new technological advancements with new challenges ahead. The new Hi-tech and sophisticated equipment and facilities are required with highly specialized training. There is need for better facilities at grass root level to produce better players. State of the art infrastructure and equipments should be provided at college and University level. Unfortunately play fields with systematic surfaces and gymnastics fitted with latest equipment are not available in our universities as yet. It is because of lack of sports facilities and competition in the country our top Indian sports person yet goes oversees for training. Ministry of sports and AIU should help the universities to build these facilities at home, developing sports infrastructure in the country. It is only after independence that some systematic efforts were made for making sports more relevant to the needs of the society. Unfortunately international level facilities are not available for our players till today.

Economical condition of colleges\universities is not very sound. Universities are dependent of colleges for revenue. Because a large number of Indian populations are poor, students and parents can not be over burdened for additional funds. We have seen that most of our players come from low income families. They cannot afford to purchase latest equipment which is very costly in the Indian market. Due to lack of modern facilities available to the college\university players, lot of talent is going waste. To achieve better results at the national and international level we must concentrate on the young players from colleges. Latest equipment should be imported by the Government and provided to the young players.

5. Sports Infrastructure and Physical Education Teachers

Physical education teachers are the real architect who are controlling and organizing at the grass root level Physical education teachers must be given proper recognition at the university level to improve the standard of sports in the universities. They should be treated at par with other teachers while framing any other sports policy for the universities. The government should associate university director with decision making committees. University director have the practical knowledge because they are working in the field. Government should make use of the technical knowledge of the sports directors to make its sports policies a success.

6. Club Culture

Indian athletes do well at home and fare badly at international meets. Usually players practice only for 3 to 4 months in a year, that is, before the inter-college and Inter-university competition. They stop their practice after these competitions are over. The fitness level they have achieved in that year comes to Zero level after they leave their training. Again they start practice before the intercollegiate competition the next year and till the end of the Interuniversity competition only. It means every year university players start from zero level fitness. Whereas level of fitness, should increase every year and reach the highest level in three to four years in the colleges. University players should maintain the level of fitness the year-round. It is possible through off season training. Club culture should be started if our player have to achieve excellence in sports. If Clubs are farmed at college and university level our players will get the chance to continue their game even after their exams are over. Physical education teachers and University players will remain in practice through out the year. They will get more inter-club competition. It will improve their performance also. If our players wish to achieve in sports they have to join such club and get themselves in-perfect fitness.

7. Conclusion

Sports and physical education are important extra-curricular facility in the education system. Basically they guide physical fitness and train the students to excel in sports in the national and international level. The new sophisticated technological equipments and facilities are needed. Managing and administering sports is challenge to the Physical Education tutors.

APPENDIX

ORGANISING COMMITTEE

Chief Patron	:	Dr. Veerendra Heggade
Patrons	:	Sri. Surendra Kumar Prof. S. Prabhakar Sri Harshendra Kumar Prof. N. Vajrakumar
Chairman	:	Dr. D.P. Giridhar
Convener	:	Dr. S.S. Bhavikatti
Co-Convener	:	Prof. C.M. Koti Dr. N.H. Ayachit
Treasurer	:	Prof. C.S. Dattatreya
Steering Committee	:	Dr. Shashidhar S. Bhavikatti Prof. I.G. Mugali Dr. S.G. Bhavi Prof. B. S. Shreeshailan Dr. C.D. Lakkannavar Dr. H.G. Gopal Sri K.D. Nadgouda Sri G.H. Joshi Sri S.P. Algur Dr. M.V. Latte
Technical Committee	:	Prof. V.N. Sukumar – Chairman Sri A.V. Kulkarni – Convener Sri K.C. Shinde Sri M.R. Kappali Sri S.G. Joshi

Smt. Vijaya C.
Dr. S.S. Joshi
Smt. Savitri Raju

Program Coordination Committee and Stage Decoration:
Dr. S.G. Bhavi – Chairman
Sri V.K. Parvati – Convener
Sri K.V. Pramod
Sri D.S. Bhat
Sri R.M. Yadahalli

Publication Committee:
Dr. A.V. Shivapur – Chairman
Dr. Vinayak Bankapur – Convener
Sri M.S. Patil
Dr. V.S. Hegde
Dr. S.S. Joshi
Sri R.C. Biradar
Sri K. Gopinath
Sri S.B. Karajgi

Transportation, Guest Hospitality & Catering Committee:
Sri Dinesh Ballulaya – Chairman
Sri Rajbansi R.L. - Convener
Sri D.S. Bhat
Sri Satish S. Desai
Sri Raghavendra Rao
Sri S.K. Dhulkhed
Dr. A.R. Desai
Sri V.K. Heblikar
Sri I.T. Shirkol
Sri P.B. Joshi
Sri U.P. Kulkarni
Sri R.S. Bahuguni
Sri Udayakumar S.

Reception : Smt J.C. Karur
Smt. Nita Kulkarni
Dr. Neeraja Rani
Smt. Rekha V. Dundur
Smt. Lokeshwari Navalgund

Publicity Committee: Dr. Vinayak Bankapur
Sri K.C. Shinde
Sri K. Gopinath
Sri G.A. Bidkar
Sri G.D. Kamalapur
Sri G.H. Joshi
Sri Ravindra Dastikop
Sri V.K. Parvati

INDEX

❑❑❑

❑❑❑